Do they eat soup in England?

Insights and advice for expats struggling to find their identity abroad

Helen McClure

Copyright © 2019 Helen McClure
All rights reserved.

What is this book about?

Are you an expat, thinking of becoming an expat, or have been an expat?

There are lots of books offering advice on *how* to be an expat: how to find schools, work, deal with rules and regulations.

This book is different. This book will support you on your emotional journey. It's like a hot bowl of soup on a cold night, designed to be an expat's friend, understanding your feelings and concerns.

This isn't a memoir or a story about a privileged sector of society. It's a series of insights into a journey affecting millions of people. A journey that can require strength, open-mindedness and patience.

But it's a wonderful journey, and the opportunity to travel and create unique experiences. You may feel cut adrift and not sure which way to row. We're all in the same boat. Welcome aboard.

Based on international expat case studies, survey results, personal experience, and wider research, this book is a ready-made personal support network, offering witty, and often poignant, insights into this special community.

Ally, a Canadian who lived in Dubai:

I didn't think about the emotional journey I was embarking on. This book would really have helped me come to terms with conflicting and confusing feelings. I just jumped straight in, but I splashed around for a bit. This book is the life buoy I needed.

Lisa, an American living in Germany

I wish I had been given this book when my husband was offered his new job. I felt so unsupported by his company. It would have made me realise that what I was experiencing was a normal part of the process. I so nearly gave up and came home.

Acknowledgements

Dedicated to my Mam, Joan, for holding my hand every step of the way; for my Dad, Steve, who gave me the strength and confidence to put one foot in front of the other, and keep going; my husband, Andy, my partner in travel and in life, keeping me sane; and to my wonderful daughters, Madeleine and Tilda, for your craziness and energy.

I love you all, wherever you are.

I would like to extend a big thank you to the hundreds of expats around the world who have helped and supported me. You have been the people that have made this book possible, giving me an insight into your expat lives.

A special mention goes to Claire, Tory, Amanda, Amy, Caroline, Allison, Justin, Becs, Angie, Josephine, Jon, Karen, Jacqueline, Norma and Niki for your time and candour.

Do they eat soup in England?

Contents

Who are the expats?..9
Family………………………………...……… 15
Friends……………………………………..… 23
Children………………………………….…. 33
Personal identity…………………………… 43
Communicating……………………………. 51
Work……………………………………...………59
Technology……………………………….…. 69
Health…………………………………….…. 77
Women……………………………………... 87
Emotions…………………………………….. 95
National identity………………………….... 103
Location connections……………………… 113
Packing up………………………………….. 125
Repating……………………………………. 135
Epilogue………………………………….. 147
Appendix…………………………………... 149
- Expat statistics…………………….. 151
- Expat extra………………………... 165
- Interview with my children…….. 169

Who are the expats?

It was a wise person who said that we are all the same, with two arms, two legs and a head, but at the same time we are all different. That person was my daughter, who was five at the time. That's the impact an expat life can have on a child, and if she remembers nothing else about her time abroad, I hope she continues to understand that we are all different races, religions and culture. And that's what makes the world an amazing place.

I want this book to be like a comfortable pair of slippers, a mug of soup on a winter's day or a hug from a friend. Whether you've been an expat, are an expat or are thinking of becoming an expat, there are as many experiences as there are people. How you frame it is unique to you. However, there are some common themes, which I've attempted to explore in this book. As you read, I hope there are moments when you think: "Yes! Someone gets me," or "Aha! So that's why I feel like this."

In researching this book, I've been privileged to meet expats and repats[1] from all over the world, with a wealth of experience. The extracts and case studies I've shared offer as many different perspectives as possible.

Two years ago, I started on a journey to try to map out who the audience to this book might be – who are the thousands of people around the world who live and work in a country that is different from the one they were born in. What is an expat, and what is the true definition?

---

[1] Repatriate.

The word *expat* is a contraction of *expatriate*, derived from the Latin *expatriare (ex = out, patria = native country)*. There is an entirely separate debate surrounding the difference between an expat and a migrant - fodder for a rather different book. Is one professional and the other not? Is one fleeing from something or searching for something? Are you pushed into it, or does it pull you in? Does it have to be for economic reasons? How many people are expats? Can there ever be any accurate statistics when the definition is so blurred?

Few, if any, of these questions have straight answers. The number of expats, for example, is difficult to quantify as few countries keep statistics. The United Nations estimates the total number of international migrants to be around 258 million, up from 220 million in 2010 and 173 million in 2000[2]. We're part of a very big family.

If the total global population is estimated to be around 7.7 billion[3] then 3.4% of people are not living in their country of origin. The number will continue to grow as globalisation continues. Scarce human resources and skills are redistributed according to local economic needs.

For the purposes of this book, the term *expat* refers to anyone, male or female, who finds themselves in a different country, without having emigrated permanently.

---

[2] http://www.un.org/en/development/desa/population/migration/publications/migrationreport/docs/MigrationReport2017_Highlights.pdf
[3] http://www.un.org/en/development/desa/population/events/pdf/other/21/21June_FINAL%20PRESS%20RELEASE_WPP17.pdf

What happens when you become an expat?

I've surveyed nearly 700 people[4] across the world and concluded that the biggest relocation issue affecting expats is the loss of their personal support network. It takes time to discover how you fit into your new home. It takes time to find the right friends. In a country full of expats, it's easy to make friends, but the turnover can be high. Countries with little experience of expats can be insular and may not appear welcoming. This is unsettling.

According to InterNations, 49% of expats and 84% of "trailing spouses" are women[5], indicating that most international moves are driven by economic factors, when considering the male/female labour split.

Working expats can enjoy a readymade support network and familiar structure at work. Children have the same at school. The homemaker often finds themselves drifting, unable to make sense of unfamiliar feelings. Everything seems like a battle, from driving on the "wrong" side of the road, to finding your local supermarket.

Some people thrive on change. They are not victims of circumstance, but enablers.

Who am I to write this book?

I understand what it's like to work abroad. I'm a trained newspaper journalist and travel writer whose work has featured in British broadsheets and various travel publications around the globe. I'm

---
[4] 675 people took part in the Expat Explorers' survey between 2016 and 2018.
[5] https://www.internations.org/magazine/the-trailing-spouse-gender-roles-abroad-15283

the founder of a non-commercial travel and expat website called Expat Explorers.

I understand the stress of children, including one who has a life-threatening condition. I'm the mother of two beautiful daughters, who were aged only two years and six months when we first moved abroad. It's not easy moving to a new country with a hyperactive toddler in one hand and a wriggling baby under your arm, when your husband has already started work and is not there to help you.

I understand the impact expat life has on children – I was an expat in Kuwait as a child. The experience gave me the automatic acceptance of different cultures that only a child can have.

I understand what it's like to move multiple times. I've lived in one of the coldest parts of the world (Chicago), one of the hottest (United Arab Emirates) and one of the most humid (Singapore).

I understand what it's like to move abroad with your partner's work, several times, usually when you've just got everyone settled.

I understand the flexibility these multiple roles demand, and the opportunities.

That is why I've written this book. I have been the expat, stunned and overwhelmed. I have girded my loins before putting my foot on the accelerator to join the crazy traffic and erratic driving styles. I have sat at home, staring at the middle distance while small children demand and cry, tugging at my trousers. I have been that women who has looked longingly at the bottle of wine, wondering when it would be acceptable to open it. I've also been the woman who has embraced everything thrown at me. Memories and life experiences are made from this stuff.

So, in summary, as a family we've tried to make the most of every opportunity to travel and learn about the world we live in, and we've had great fun doing so. It's a story about a journey millions of people take. It requires strength, when all you feel is doubt. It requires open-mindedness, when you suffer a loss of confidence. It requires patience, when you're wrapped up in red tape and about to hang yourself.

But it's a wonderful journey, and the opportunity to create unique experiences.

Happy travels!
Helen

Helen McClure
helen@expatexplorers.org

Do they eat soup in England?

Family

Nearly half of all expats cite being close to family as what they miss most when living abroad[6], and nearly 60% of expats move abroad with children[7]. Whether it's parents, children or siblings that you leave behind, the aching void created is very difficult to fill with online chats and emails. Technology has made things a little easier, but it has also raised the expectations of family members. It's difficult to put yourself in each other's shoes. The ones at home are not forgotten, but time differences, unreliable broadband and the trials of settling in a new place are challenges.

It's also hard to reassure family members who don't understand why you moved. They often seem to take the news personally, as if their love isn't enough to stop you from going.

I was lucky. This was not a pressure I had to face when I first moved abroad as an adult. My parents had moved us to Kuwait in the Middle East when I was seven, a place few had even heard of in 1982. My grandparents generally accepted that you had to move with work, having struggled to make ends meet. They understood that most people are hostages of the pay-packet when you have a young family to support.

I vividly remember my parents' efforts to try and stay in contact from afar. We didn't have a phone in our flat, so made arrangements with a neighbour on special occasions, but knowing my parents, they probably didn't want to inconvenience others too

---

[6] Expat Explorers' survey: 46% of respondents said that family is what they missed most about home. A further 17% said that friends were what they missed most.

[7] Expat Explorers' survey: 59% of respondents had children; 28% lived with just a partner; 7% were independent; 2% lived with their parents.

often. A part solution to this was a tape recorder. My brother, sister and I were invited to say hello into the machine, or sing a song, often with my three-year-old brother just nodding inaudibly.

When it was my mother's turn we were not only banished from the room, but from the flat, in an effort to try to ease her anguish of having to have a conversation with an inanimate object.

As an adult, I can't say I've been very successful at staying in regular contact with friends and family while living abroad. The intent is there, but in my defence I come from an upbringing of "no news is good news".

My biggest emotional challenge came when we lived in Singapore and my father was diagnosed with cancer. It's a huge heartache and a scar that will never heal. I wanted to spend as much time with him as possible, knowing that the prognosis was not good. But how do you do that without stifling the ones you love, your temporary undivided attention only underlining the gravity of the situation?

I also had the challenge of two small children to look after, and an endless list of questions about how everyone would cope without me. I'd missed the point of life though. It wasn't about whether the girls went to school with their hair neatly in bunches, and a healthy meal on the table every evening. It wasn't about the cost of the flight and the unknown. It was about emotional connection, and the children, my husband and my parents, knowing that they were loved. Above all, I felt torn and guilty that I couldn't be everything and everywhere for everyone.

With the support of friends and helpers, I flew back to the UK to spend two weeks on my own with my parents, wrenching tearful children off my legs as I tried to clamber into the taxi taking me to the airport. It was precious time. I told my father I was coming home to investigate schools as we were hoping to move home. He never said he didn't believe me, but there was little evidence as I spent the days talking to him and going for short walks. It would have made him feel so uncomfortable to know that he was the reason I was home on my own, even though I'm sure he did know.

Two weeks after I flew back to Singapore my father's health rapidly deteriorated to the point that he was asking for me. I immediately boarded a plane home, and helped nurse him at home with my mother. He died ten days later. He was only 67.

Technology may have shrunk our world, but it's still very difficult to bounce 14 hours across the world. The fact that you're not available to help when needed leads to guilt, and often puts a greater share of the burden on family and friends at home.

People who are not expats generally think that your life is gilded. Warmer weather and cocktails epitomise expat life to some, supported by jolly photos on Facebook. After all, you rarely take pictures in the rain, so your life always appears sunny. However, all expats know that grass isn't always greener on the other side. Of course, there are advantages, but the emotional tug of family is hard to bear.

Meet Claire

Claire, a Brit who has lived in Singapore, found herself between a rock and a hard place with expat life causing difficulties for her family, whether she moved to a new country or returned home.

It takes a certain type of person with an inner strength to become an expat. For some it's not even a move they will consider, and sometimes it's easy to see why.

I remember driving to my parents' house to tell them that we were moving away. I sat down with my father and the response was "Well, that's f***ed up the evening." He just turned back to the television and didn't speak to me for the rest of the evening. He was so bitter that I was going to take his grandchildren away. I had broken his heart. It was one of the worst moments of my life.

I drove home in tears. We were moving with my husband's job, but I hadn't considered my feelings to be honest. I just didn't expect to be embarking on such a wonderful journey with such a mixed bag of emotions. I realised just how much of a sacrifice I would have to make. I was not averse to the idea of living abroad for a few years and I was excited that we had been given an opportunity to really explore and become a part of a completely different way of life. I just wished that my parents had supported that decision. Losing your grandchildren, one at the delightful age of four and the other just finding her feet in the world at 18 months, was of course going to be heart wrenching. In the months leading up to our departure they did give me their blessing, but they had to. We are a close family and they wanted me to be happy.

Every visit we made back home ended in trauma, putting on brave faces when it was time to return to the airport, and I lived with this amazing guilt. This was made all the more acute when my mother found out she had breast cancer, while I was living in Singapore. I wasn't there for her.

After three years, I suggested to my husband that it was time to go home. He asked me to give it one more year. Then another year. After five years I had had enough.

One day he came home and dumped a package on the table and said: "There you go. That's the one-way tickets for you and the children." He had decided to stay in Singapore and felt he didn't have a choice. The growth for his industry was in Asia, and hence his business is doing so well now. There just weren't the job opportunities to come back to.

So, again I was left with the terrible guilt of leaving. I broke my parents' heart to support my husband and then I broke my husband's heart to return home.

For the past five years my husband and I have been living in different countries. We're still together, but he commutes back and forth from Asia, having gone on to set up his own business out there. We live a split family lifestyle. I have the strength, most of the time, to bring up three children on my own, but I did not foresee what a heart wrenching, unsettling world it could become. Expat lifestyles can put a strain on even the strongest of marriages.

What other expats have to say

Amy, a Brit living in Argentina

Saying "goodbye" to friends and family when they have come to visit is always hard. My sons have all been through a phase of refusing to say "goodbye" to people when they leave, believing that in not doing so, the individuals will stay!

Meet Joan

When our daughter announced she was going to live in Chicago, my husband and I were anguished with mixed emotions. We would miss all of them especially our only two grandchildren, then aged two years and six months, an age when they are funny and growing fast.

Who were we to complain? We had done exactly the same to our parents 30 years ago. Our experiences gave us the inside knowledge. We knew that life abroad would enrich their lives.

Five years and three countries later they still live abroad, and we have had some wonderful holidays staying with them. Our arrival is always kept a secret from the grandchildren, so the highlight of our stay is their faces when they open the door and see us standing there. The first cuddle is the most wonderful thing.

Living with the family enables us to spend quality time with them, reading books, going to their school and meeting their friends, and being shown new places through a child's eye. They know no different, so they are both curious and accepting. They are not on holiday, so we try to fit in with the normal family routine enjoying the different ways of doing things. This wonderful time is always paid for in tears when we have to say goodbye.

Darren, Brit who lived in the US

I moved back to the UK to be closer to family, and then my (only) brother emigrated to Canada. That was a bit irritating.

Where do you start?

- Write a list of the most important people in your life and email or text them to say hello. A "little and often" approach can go a long way.

- Set up appointments or virtual coffees so you have dates in your diary to look forward to.

- Send a postcard. It may be old-fashioned, but everyone loves a positive note through the letterbox, rather than a bill.

- Remember birthdays and anniversaries. There is often an out of sight, out of mind mentality, but just by showing you care can help to build, or even rebuild, relationships.

Friends

One of the biggest issues of moving abroad is separating yourself from your support network - you feel like you are on your own. Nearly 15% of expats think the new distance from friends is the main disadvantage of expat life[8]. However, more than three-quarters (76%) said they found it easy to make friends.

If you are the sort of person who gathers loved ones around you, going from a comfortable friendship group to being among total strangers can be a dramatic change in lifestyle that is really tricky to deal with. The contrast can be as stark as leaving a busy, bustling, noisy, active nightclub, straight to sitting in a tiny boat, bobbing about on the ocean with no idea which direction to row. The silence is deafening, and you know you can't just sit there. You have to do something. But what?

The positive side of this situation is that all expats are in the same boat, or have been. It's also a small boat. The expat society isn't huge, and every expat knows what it's like to land on foreign shores clueless, and perhaps a bit lonely. That is what makes expats so open and welcoming. You just have to ask for help.

However, while some cultures are full of expats all supporting each other, other locations are a little more problematic. With a young family, I didn't find our first move abroad easy. In the freezing depths of winter, we landed in the outer suburbs of Chicago, an area that had little experience or interest in transient neighbours.

---

[8] Expat Explorers' survey: Of a total of 675 survey respondents to the question "What do you miss the most about home?" 47% missed family, 15% cited friends, 10% stated countryside, 3% said weather. A further 2% missed their working life.

My husband disappeared off to work, leaving me at home with the ubiquitous towers of cardboard boxes, a baby and a toddler. We had chosen to live in a leafy, spacious suburb, attracted by the climbing frames in the garden. After all, climbing frames meant children, which meant young families like us. Except in this case it didn't. It meant empty nesters, with climbing frames for the occasional visit from grandchildren.

I almost resented my husband's position. He had the recognisable structure of work to anchor him. He had people to talk to and could have intellectually interesting conversations. I love my children, but as babies they weren't exactly chatty.

I felt I was stuck in the middle of nowhere. I had to drive everywhere as nothing was in walking distance. In the depths of a Mid-West winter, in freezing temperatures of -30C, just getting out of the house was a huge challenge with young children. I'd put on their jumpers, coats, snow suits and boots, then hot and bothered get myself dolled up – then one of the girls would need their nappy changing, and the dressing rigmarole would be reversed. This routine could occur several times before I actually managed to get them in the car – and then I would need the loo. This often left me little time to go out and meet people.

Sometimes, countries with a limited experience of expats can be insular and may not appear welcoming. No-one can accuse the US of not being friendly, but a conversation about your interesting accent in a queue at the post office is not equivalent to a dinner invitation.

It takes time to find friends. My first contact with people my own age was through a baby and toddler group. A lovely bunch of girls, but I needed more than conversations about nappies. Although a guilty decision, I found a lovely nursery for the girls to attend two mornings a week, while I went back to college to study interior design. I wanted to make the most of living abroad, see as much as possible, and dig deep to discover how the place ticked. Chicago is a wonderful city, full of dramatic architecture and full-bodied Mid-West culture.

A country full of expats is the polar opposite. It's easy to make friends, but not so easy to get to grips with the local culture if you live in your expat bubble. The turnover of expats can also be high. After Chicago, we moved to Dubai and then on to Singapore, two communities with huge expat populations. Immediately, I was able to connect with like-minded people. Friendships were formed quickly, everyone understanding the transient nature of expat life. Hearts were frequently broken, and tears shed when friends moved on, however. The danger is that if you don't cast your social net further, you don't get to know the local population, and your involvement in local culture is restricted. You don't immerse yourself. You observe from afar. But cultural enrichment was the top reason given as an advantage of expat life[9].

Friends help to enhance expat life, sharing knowledge and creating memories. Just being aware of the type of culture you are moving into can help. Is it a peach or a coconut? Modern societies, such as the US, are peach cultures. They are soft and welcoming, but with a harder inner core that may make it more difficult to be accepted. The reverse is true of the UK. By comparison it is a formal society. People can appear stand-offish, while they wait for an introduction, not wanting to intrude. It has a hard outer shell, but once you're through, you make friends for life. Neither is better than the other, but just part of the diverse fruit bowl of life.

---

[9] Expat Explorers' survey: Top three advantages of expat life = Cultural experience (32%), financially better off (26%), travel (16%)

Meet Tory

Tory is a Brit who is pretty much an expat expert, having lived in South Africa until the age of 13, returning to live there with a young family. She's also lived in Dubai twice, and is now packing up for new horizons in the Netherlands.

Moving around the world with your family is a double-edge sword. It's wonderful to have friends all over the globe, enabling you to experience different cultures from the inside. I have met some incredible people and have made some life-long friendships. As I keep telling my girls, when they are old enough to travel the world on their own, they will know at least one person on each continent!

However, even with the advanced technology of today, it can be tricky staying in touch. I have certainly lost some good friends. You can't, or more realistically, don't share your day to day life so easily when you live across the world from each other, and it's often these little things that bond you together.

The lives of my British friends at home have moved on in a totally different way to mine, and this sometimes causes a gap were there never was before. Having said that, I do have some friends from university that I may only see for a few days each year, or sometimes a couple of years may go by, but I know they will always be there for me and vice versa. Interestingly enough, when I think about it, these friends have generally also lived abroad at some point in their lives, or have close family members that do.

It is easier, in some ways, to stay friends with those that you have met along the way – whether you have moved, they have moved on themselves or gone 'back home'. These are the friends that you may not speak to for months, but when you do it's like you saw them yesterday and easily carry on from where you left off. You have common ground and a unique understanding of each other.

The best bit of advice I received, when we first moved, was that the first four months are crucial. It's really important to get involved with much as possible - meet as many people as you can, just get out and about before you begin to settle into a routine. The first time we moved, my girls were younger; it was exciting; it was a hot country; it was a culture I had never experienced.

As the children get older it gets harder to make friends. You no longer wait outside the classroom at the end of the day, a prime time to meet other parents; you are no longer needed, or wanted, to attend playdates or wait while they do an extra activity – another great time to drink coffee and get to know parents in the same situation. To be honest, I have adopted this advice less and less with each consecutive move. I've found as I have got older, I have also got pickier about whom I want to spend my time with, and would sometimes prefer to sit in a coffee shop with a good book, than chat to someone I don't have much in common with or don't know!!

One conversation I have had many times is where you call 'home', or where you feel your true roots are. We have always said that our home is where we are. Our family of five (and two dogs) is 'home'. It doesn't matter which country we are in. If we are together that's what counts. I'm sure this will get harder as the kids get older and then I guess it comes down to where the family home is. It's the place they come back to.

I'm no longer sure I know where my 'home' is. I can't give a definitive answer. Most of my family, my Dad and brothers, are in the UK, but I certainly don't feel a pull to be there. Being brought up in South Africa for the first 13 years of my life, I never really regarded UK as home anyway and always swore I would leave some day. It was only once I was married and had children that I felt settled and the need to go elsewhere diminished.

Dubai is very much an expat community with people frequently talking about 'home' as the country they've originated from. Living in Dubai is a temporary state, no matter how long you have lived here. I find this quite unsettling. Living in South Africa, as an expat, however, was very different. We took a conscious decision to surround ourselves with local South Africans. The girls went to the local schools rather than an international school, and although we lived in very much an expat community, our main friends were outside of this.

Although many South Africans have strong ties to other countries, South Africa is their home. I think because of this, and the fact that I had called it 'home' for the first part of my life, it very quickly became just that. In some ways, I think it will always remain so, over and above UK, even for my girls who only lived there for four years.

Our next move will take us to Amsterdam. This will be another totally different experience, having lived in a 'developing' market for the past eight years. How we settle, and how we make friends, will be influenced by our decision to buy a house, instead of renting. It will have a bearing on the community we live in and how we are linked to the community.

We'll be selling our house in the UK, which is currently rented out, removing a large tie to the country. Who knows what the next few years will hold for us, but I do know, or hope, that we will meet some more amazing people along the way.

What other expats have to say

Rebecca, from Australia, has lived in Malaysia and India
I met some of the best people I'll ever meet, and love that I have friends all over the world who we still see and keep in contact with.

Jacqueline, a Brit, has 20 years of experience as an expat, living in the UAE, Australia, New Zealand and Hong Kong
Being an expat makes people transient, long term friendship are rarer, but those made survive over decades.

Devin, an American living in Saudi Arabia
My husband and I were trying to have children while abroad, because I was not working and could stay home with no financial impact. We finally got pregnant six months later. We had a miscarriage when visiting Abu Dhabi. Our friends were supportive and helped me through the grief while being so far from family. It made me realise how close some people were and how much I had in common with others that I never thought.

Meet Kim

Kim is an Australian who has lived in Singapore, Papua New Guinea and the Philippines.

We met our best friends 20 years ago. My hubby had just moved to Papua New Guinea, and the kids and I were busy packing up house.

He was staying in the local hotel. One night the fire alarm went off and everyone evacuated the hotel, standing around lost. He started chatting to a family of a husband, wife and three-month-old baby. It was late, they were all tired, but they kept each other company, amused and eventually exchanged numbers.

Roll on six months. I'd been living in Papua New Guinea a few months, and my hubby invited the family he'd met to a ball so I could meet them. We had fun, clicked and organised a Thursday afternoon drinks.

Thursday became Fridays (it's too hard getting kids to school on a Friday after a Thursday drinking session – I found that out the hard way!). Friday sessions grew with more new friends being invited.

Now 20 years later we have a core of five very special friends – the FADLs (Friday Afternoon Drinking Ladies!). We live in different parts of the world/country yet catch up whenever we can. And when we do, it's just like old times. It's like no time has passed between us. They are my best friends!

Amanda, an American living in the UK

Visiting home is an interesting emotional journey. While you're living aboard you experience life changes at a different pace than your friends – they are no longer chapters of life that you go through together. We left the US as a couple with a vibrant social life and tons of freedom. Then we had children. And we aged! So, we're different now, and we're different from how people remember us. When we visit the US, I sometimes feel like old friends are a little disappointed that we don't have quite the nightlife we used to. Unless you count being up with children in the middle of the night as a nightlife.

Lucy, a Brit living in Singapore

I was stuck at the school coffee shop three weeks after moving. I looked around and figured I could sit by myself or just walk up to a table and introduce myself. I did the latter and found a wonderful friend who has been supportive and given me lots of help and advice. People back home don't understand the [expat] way of life and can become resentful and jealous. You need to understand their point of view but enjoy what you have.

Where do you start?

- It sounds obvious, but keep in contact with friends at home as often as possible, even if it is just the odd text. It makes visits home much easier and less awkward. Your relationship will probably not be the same but you'll have built other memories with them, just by staying in touch.

- The Christmas family newsletter might not be everyone's cup of tea, but when you live abroad people are genuinely interested in what turns your life has taken. Make sure you keep copies as they make super reminders and mementoes for your children.

- The school gate is a great place to strike up conversation. You may just have your situation and the fact that you have children in common though. Think about your hobbies and past-times and join clubs to meet people with similar interests. Or learn a new skill. How about taking up calligraphy or having tennis lessons?

- Be proactive and start your own gathering. It doesn't have to a be a huge society. Create a book club with a few neighbours that starts with a glass of wine and some canapes. Put up a poster in your apartment block or condo asking all runners to unite. Invite a few friends to an American supper where everyone brings a dish from their home country.

Children

When you take the giant leap and move to another country and culture, one of the biggest worries is often how the children will cope. However, nearly 60% of people move abroad with children[10], and more than 60% of families have pre-school aged children[11]. Hours have been spent fretting over whether they will make friends, deal with a new language, like the food, cope with the weather.

Funnily enough they often settle quicker than adults[12]. They don't have any preconceived ideas about what their new life is going to be like, so they don't tend to worry, they just accept. School-aged children have a recognisable structure in the form of their educational establishment, and younger children are too young to be bothered as long as they are with their family.

The lack of awareness, in terms of other cultures, can often get you into hot water, however. Little children will cross unwritten barriers, naturally lacking the social skills and moral code of grown-ups. Where adults see these barriers as twelve-foot brick walls with barbed wire on top, to children they are imperceptible. This is evidenced by the funny, endearing and often cringe-worthy things they say.

Most expats try to make the most of life abroad, and travelling with

---

[10] Expat Explorers' survey: 59% of respondents had children; 28% lived with just a partner; 7% were independent; 2% lived with their parents.
[11] Expat Explorers' survey: 60% of families had pre-school aged children; 26% had primary school aged children; 6% had secondary school aged children; 7% adult children.
[12] Expat Explorers' survey: People overwhelming thought that children benefitted from expat life (96%), with multicultural experience and open mindedness being cited as positive reasons. However, 49% still thought there were challenges, such as distance from family and instability.

young children can be an education in itself. People are interested in talking to two blond, curly-haired children in a land where everyone has black hair. They are a curiosity and open the door to conversations with locals, which in turn gives you a new perspective.

Add this to their childish observations, and you have a multi-faceted experience.

The title of this book is based on something my younger daughter, Tilda, asked when we moved from Singapore back to the UK. We had left Britain when she was six-months-old, so she had no idea what it was like other than from holidays. It was natural for her to enquire whether soup was available on the British menu.

Expat life also offers children an introduction to other religions. When Madeleine was five, I decided to test her knowledge:

Me: "Madeleine, if you want to pray where would you go?"
Madeleine: "You could go to a mosque, a church or a temple."
Me: "Just out of interest, how do you pray?"
Madeleine: "You get a bit of carpet and you kiss the floor."

I didn't say what children absorb is always understood, but it's an interesting insight. I need to make sure she doesn't take a prayer mat with her next time she goes to church parade with the Brownies.

Here's another cherished moment with my children:

Me: "Will you still give me cuddles like this when you're an adult?"
Madeleine (aged 8): "Well, no, because I'll be living in a different country."
Me: "You are allowed to live in the same country."
Madeleine: "Oh."

Tilda (age 5): "I want to live in the same house, except that won't be possible."
Me: "Why?"
Tilda: "You'll be dead."

Charming. Let's assume she is aware of the natural demise of humans, rather than developing a plot to get her hands on the inheritance.

Meet Amanda

Amanda, an American, gave birth to her two children in Dubai, and then moved to the UK. Intrigued with the way they see the world, she hopes their expat experience will give them a broad acceptance of the world, while still understanding their place in it.

When we moved to Dubai, I gave up my career to support my husband's promotional opportunity. I arrived in a new country and culture without a plan for myself, but having a family seemed to be the natural step, especially as Dubai is family-friendly. Leaving my career was hard to do at the time, but it's been a wonderful experience and allows us great flexibility as a family.

I was lucky to have both my children in a country with excellent quality private healthcare. While many women choose to return to their home country for birth, that wasn't an option for me due to a 17-hour flight and high-risk pregnancies.

Identity has been the main issue with having the children in a country where they don't have citizenship. Our only option was to pursue the citizenship of our home country for our children. Given the option, we would have pursued dual citizenship as this would have given the girls a link to their cultural identity. They are technically Americans, but they have never lived there. We now live in the UK, and they may feel British, just like the other children at their school. I want them to feel a belonging to the country if that's important to them.

When people ask what nationality they are I generally describe them as culturally confused. Time will tell. My little one was five-weeks-old when we moved from Dubai to the UK. My older daughter remembers life in Dubai, but has spent the last 18 months in the British school system. She knows she sounds different to her classmates and when people ask her why, she tells them she's an Arab. She has both a broad and incredibly narrow sense of culture all at the same time!

I honestly believe the children have a good life abroad and wonderfully enriching opportunities. I don't want them to feel different their whole lives. I don't want them to feel different from their peers living abroad and then feel different to Americans if we move back there. We're trying to find a balance. Their cultural experience will be different, but not necessarily better or worse. They might know different television shows or music or foods to their peers in the US, but those aren't things that matter.

I think they'll have an interesting story to tell, hopefully making them unique, accepting, adventurous, compassionate people. I also think they'll have an expanded view of "home". Home is where I live and contribute, but not necessarily where I'm from. Home is the dining room table where I have breakfast with my parents and do my homework, and that sense of home can exist anywhere.

The main disadvantage to expat life is the instability. We don't know how long we're going to live somewhere and where we're going next. I've tried to let go of that worry. We'll land exactly where we're supposed to. The last four relocations have proven that. We've loved every place we've called home for different reasons. But I imagine it's going to get harder as the children get older and their friendship groups and interests are established. I just don't want them to feel displaced or lonely. People who have lived in the same place their whole lives find expat instability hard to understand and swallow. I see it as part of the adventure. Where we go next, and when, is a mystery, so we'll enjoy life in this spot for as long as we're here. We will make it our home, even if it's temporary.

The other primary disadvantage is the distance from family. Our children don't get to see grandparents, aunts, uncles, cousins and friends nearly as much as we'd like. I'm grateful for FaceTime and Skype, but it doesn't replace a hug or a bedtime story on Grandma's lap.

It's interesting to try to see your expat life through the eyes of your children. They don't see cultural differences as a benefit of being an expat.

They don't see themselves as different. They just accept people, regardless of their race or religion, and that's what makes all the struggles worthwhile.

What other expats have to say

Jane, a Brit, has lived in Indonesia, Cyprus, Singapore
Flying around the world as an unaccompanied child, and in charge of a younger brother, was scary, and left me with a desire to bring my own children up in one lovely country home. It left my brother with a permanent desire to travel!

Andy, a Brit, has lived in the US, UAE and Singapore
You can't help but feel proud when your eight-year-old daughter has a conversation in Mandarin with a taxi driver. You can't help but be intrigued by watching your six-year-old daughter struggle to answer the apparently simple question: "Where are you from?"

Ali, a Brit, has lived in Egypt, South Africa, Philippines, Thailand, France and Singapore
I grew up as an expat brat but was sent to boarding school in the UK at age 11. During my first weekend at school, at breakfast, I looked at the selection of jars and sauces, which were permanently on a shelf. I chose mint sauce for my toast. My peers looked at me wide-eyed but said nothing... and watched me gag as I ate two slices. I still get teased about it to this day.

Karien, Dutch, living in Singapore

Be careful, your expat children are likely to end up expats themselves. I did, and so did many of my friends. It's contagious! People tend to say expat life is not 'normal' and that we live in a bubble. For me, this is normal, and I know no other life and love it.

Claire, a Brit, has lived in USA, Canada and Australia

We moved from Canada to Australia when I was 35 weeks pregnant! We didn't have any baby things, and no home to move into.

Anita, a Brit, has lived in Italy, France and UAE

When we were told we had to leave Dubai I was utterly heart broken. After a particularly sad day my then 11-year-old put her arms around me and said: "Mummy don't be sad. It's an exciting, new adventure and as long as the five of us are together we will be OK." I knew then that we had done the right thing moving around.

Joan, a Brit, is a grandmother with family in Singapore

Staying with our grandchildren opened our eyes. The children, aged seven and five, had no preconceived ideas and noticed things that would otherwise go unnoticed. It adds a new dimension to the travel experience when you have a small child as your tour guide.

Where do you start?

- Keep a log of the funny and intriguing things your children say. It will give you some insight into how they see the world.

- If you have young children, create a photobook or keep a scrapbook to give to them when they are older. It will help them to remember their expat lives.

- Encourage your children to write letters to family at home, as well as setting up phone calls to keep in touch with family at home.

- If your children are learning a new language consider encouraging them to keep it going when you return home. It may give them an educational edge or simply help them stay in contact with their expat self.

Personal identity

A strange phenomenon occurs when you move abroad - your personal identity changes. That's not to say your personality changes, but your role and environment affect how you see yourself, and how you think others see you.

If you're moving to make the most of work opportunities[13], there are several main categories you could fit into. You become an expat because:

- You have a job offer or your current employer is relocating you;

- Your partner has to move for work, which means you have to give up your career, put it on ice or negotiate a professional move;

- Your partner has to move for work, and your role is to look after the family;

- You marry someone from a different country and move aboard – although there is some debate about when you stop being an expat in this scenario;

- You move abroad for sunnier climes, for travel opportunities or to study.

The amount of control you have can have an impact on whether the

---

[13] Expat Explorer's survey: 43% moved due their partners' job prospects and 23% moved due to their own job prospects. Just over 13% moved for a cultural experience and 6% moved for financial reasons.

experience is positive or negative. Your frame of mind also has an influence, as does your age and stage in life.

For example, if you are being asked to move abroad due to your partner's job, you have little control, even though as a couple you may decide it is the right thing to do. You can choose to see yourself as the victim of the situation, the "trailing spouse", or you may frame the situation as an opportunity to travel and learn about a new culture. Even if you are a glass half full type of person, it doesn't automatically follow that the move is easy, or that you feel positive all the time. This is sometimes due to the personal identity crisis that many expats experience.

I love travelling. I love learning about new cultures. I was an expat as a child. However, that didn't stop me from having momentary blips in my confidence, because I was still scoping out my role and, therefore, my identity. We'd left the UK with my husband's job, two young children in tow. I had to put my public relations business on ice. I knew it was the right thing to do, and I could focus my energy fully on the children. I knew I was the enabler who could make relocation happen by creating a warm, safe home in a new land.

From time to time resentment did rear its ugly head, usually after a bad day. I felt like I was the only person who organised anything, and looked after the children, and kept the house clean, and worked out every detail of how to function in a foreign land, from buying vegetables to dealing with the speeding fine I'd been given during my first week of driving.

I craved intellectual stimulation. I needed to see some progression. What I needed most was some guidance on whether I was doing a good job or not, because I constantly felt like I was skating on ice, balancing a cup and saucer on my head. I asked a fellow expat friend whether she felt the same. "I'm basically the concierge," she said.

This resentment, which was always temporary, might have occurred if I had stayed in the UK. It's an issue a lot of mothers feel when they give up work to have children. There are several added dimensions, however. Everything is different, you initially have no support network and you don't know how you fit in. If I could identify with my surroundings, I could anchor myself. On average it takes expats between six and 12 months to feel settled[14].

It's surprising how much of your personal identity is inherently attached to your nationality. Therefore, when you move to an area where you are surrounded by nationalities you haven't related to before, there is a period of learning, adjustment and reframing.

The same happens when people take a DNA test to trace their ancestry. Their preconceived ideas, family knowledge and history creates biases, whether they like it or not. Take a fish out of water, and it is still a fish, it's just a very uncomfortable fish. The key is to learn how to swim out of water.

People seem to get the expat bug. Of course, there are plenty of stories of people desperate to return home. However, a survey conducted for this book[15] suggests that the average length of stay abroad is five to 10 years[16], with around 80% of expats living in more than one country[17]. Only 4% of expats returned home after a year.

When you first consider moving abroad it appears to be a gigantic step to take, and a major upheaval. Like any new situation you get

---

[14] Expat Explorers' survey: 31% of 675 respondents felt settled after 6-12 months; 19% took between three and six months; 23% took more than a year.

[15] Expat Explorers' survey of 675 respondents of 61 nationalities in 56 countries.

[16] Expat Explorers' survey: The average (mode) length of stay abroad is five to 10 years (29%). 16% have lived abroad for more than 20 years and 23% have lived aboard for less than five years. 4% of expats returned home after a year.

[17] Expat Explorers' survey: Only 19% have only lived in one country; 30% have lived in two; 26% have lived in three; 11% have lived in four; 13% have lived in more than five countries.

used to it as you adapt and adjust to different ways of living. The next move is never as daunting. Part of the acclimatisation process is a change in how you view the world and your place in it. It's about understanding who you are in your new setting. It's about finding your personal identity.

Meet Caroline

Caroline, a Brit who has lived in Malaysia and Indonesia, has just moved to Singapore with her husband's job. She understands more than most what it feels like to scrabble around trying to identify how you fit into your new home.

It takes a certain type of person with inner strength to become an expat. Some of my friends would never even consider it.

When we moved to Jakarta, in Indonesia, I felt like I had a lot to prove. The type of lifestyle you have means that you have a lot of staff. Yes, it's a nice way to live, but there is an expectation that as a Westerner you are more affluent, and therefore should be able to provide a job for a maid or a driver.

Having people working for me domestically meant I had a lot of time on my hands, but I was on the go all the time. I felt like I had a lot to prove, but I'm not sure what or to who. I think I was just trying to find my place. It was about self-preservation. I ended up running a big project developing an online relocation guide to help other expats.

Meet Amanda

Amanda, an American now living in the UK, found her personal identity was intrinsically linked to the friends she made.

When you move abroad for professional reasons, for example with a company, the focus is on the practicalities of the move; finding a house, finding schools, sorting out a driving licence or learning a language. There seems to be little practical support offered to members of the family who are moving due to circumstance.

I felt like I gave up a lot to follow my husband's career, but I never realised how much I would gain. Moving abroad has been simultaneously the most valuable and difficult experience of my life. At the top of the list of challenges is making friends.

When I moved to the Middle East, I entered a population that was full of expats and everyone was in the same boat. Then we moved to the UK, and at first I found this to be a much more difficult place to make friends than any other place I had lived previously.

It seemed like everyone had lived in the same community since birth and had a network of family and friends. There was no room for a new dodgy American friend. Thankfully, children are a great way to meet people, and school and baby playgroups have really opened the door. If not for the children, I think the move here would have been much more difficult.

Now my children are going to school in the UK, and they have British accents, and I sometimes think: "who are these little people who sounds so different to me?" It's confusing my own personal identity so goodness knows what theirs will be like.

What other expats have to say

Sara, an American who lives in Italy
Give yourself time, lots of time, to adjust. And don't make comparisons between your new home and your country of origin: they're different not comparable.

Sam, a Brit living in UAE
I love living overseas, but it took two years to find the kind of friends that I was close to, and since then I have been able to do so many things - I've learned to scuba dive, returned to horse riding, I go hiking and camping regularly. I've travelled to so many countries, many of which, in the Arab world, I never imagined I would see. I met my partner, and we enjoy a life that we would not have back in the UK. I miss the countryside and nature, but I get that in large doses when I travel. The only thing missing is friends and family.

Aimee, an Australian who lived in Singapore
Being an expat is a fun, memorable and a once-in-a-lifetime experience. The travel opportunities and people you get to meet are really life changing. But that also means you lose your sense of "home" and the longer you do it, the less you will really feel like you belong anywhere.

Where do you start?

- Give yourself time to adjust, get out often and see the sites, join local clubs/organisations to meet people. Say yes.

- Keep a diary of the good days as well as the bad, or simply write a list of the positive elements of your expat life, and the limitations. Focus on expanding the positive and be proactive. For example, if expat life has given you more free time, work out how to fill it with a new hobby, study or volunteer work.

- If you are the "concierge", you'll be running around helping your family to settle. Give yourself time too. Book a manicure, go to the library and curl up in a corner with a good book, or keep a sketch book. Don't lose sight of what makes you happy and who you are.

- Get planning. Try not to get bogged down with the day to day worries without balancing them with a bit of forward planning. Give yourself some focus and aims for the week. Plan a mini-break, learn a new local cuisine recipe or simply work out how to get from A to B.

Communicating

Learning a new language can be an exciting chance to burrow into an unknown world, unlocking new experiences and encounters. For others, not being able to converse in the same tongue can be extremely stressful, locking them out of society, holding them at arm's length. I'm not a great linguist, so to me it can feel like a cartoon scenario, where I'm a child running full pelt towards a new life, only to be held back by an adult holding my head, my legs spinning as I get nowhere fast. However, nearly a third of all expats learn a new language, successfully or not.[18]

Communication barriers don't necessarily even have to involve a foreign tongue. British English is not the same as American English for example. And Singlish is Singapore's colloquial English, modified using local languages to such an extent as to be unrecognisable to native English speakers. You say, leh! Heck it, lah! You might understand some, onz?

Cultural nuances, colloquialisms and clichéd phases are such an integral part of communication. They provide colour to words, short cuts to situations and paint double meanings you have no hope in understanding unless you are more than fluent: Unless you are local in some cases. This means you can never really understand what's going on 100% of the time, even if you've lived in one place for decades.

When I moved to Chicago, I counted my lucky stars that I didn't have to learn a new language. I had enough on my plate: I was moving to a new house for the fourth time in three years, away

---

[18] Expat Explorers' survey: 32% respondents learnt a new language.

from family across the Atlantic, with a toddler and a new baby.

I very quickly learnt that I was learning a new language. You can't go to the supermarket (grocery store) and pick up a trolley (cart), and ask for aubergines, courgettes and nappies (eggplants, zucchini and diapers). It's even tricky using the same words. I tried to ask for a glass of water and my three-year-old had to intervene and ask for "warda" as I wasn't making myself understood. People look at you blankly. And why wouldn't they? You are not speaking American.

The same happens when people visit the UK. They often have to navigate the subtleties and subtext of English. The difference is that American film and television culture has a greater global reach than British exports, which means Americans can make themselves understood more readily than Brits.

Although, would you necessarily understand what is meant when a Brit starts a sentence with: "With the greatest respect…"? You might interpret this as a respectful listening cue, when in fact the communicator is probably being derogatory.

Or how about someone nodding sagely, saying: "That's very interesting." You might think they are indeed impressed with something you've said, when really they think you're talking nonsense.

The actual spoken words are only a small part of the communication process. Add to the mix metaphors, similes, local knowledge, cultural references, vocal intonation and even hand signals and other physical gestures, and it's a wonder that we attempt to learn a new language in the first place. As expats we want to understand and be understood. We also want to avoid offence. This is sometimes harder to do.

Meet Amy

Amy is a serial expat who has spent time in Serbia, Argentina, Germany, France, Oman, Australia, New Zealand and Pakistan. She is a brilliant linguist and relishes the opportunity to learn new languages.

You develop a wonderful sense of belonging when you learn the language of your host country, and without it I think you can be rather lost. It's a mental challenge I relish, but you're always making progress and that achievement is great to see. I love the feeling when a complex grammar structure comes instinctively, and I no longer fall over my own tongue as my brain catches up. Something just clicks.

You don't have to be a good linguist, or fluent for it to open doors though. Language helps to create friendships, prevents you from being lost, and from eating delicacies you may wish to avoid. In the ice cream shop, around the corner from our house in Buenos Aires, I asked for cucarachas (cockroaches) instead of cucuruchos (cones). I'm pretty sure they weren't even on the menu!

But the more you learn, the greater your understanding of the place you're living in. I love being able to walk into a market or shop and have more than a basic exchange with the shopkeeper. The nuances, colloquialisms, hand gestures, and even obscenities, give you such an insight into the local culture.

Initially, knowing a little of the local language helps you to settle more quickly, and deeply. It stops you from feeling so isolated. There are key moments in the settling process, which help to give you the feeling that you belong, whether that's navigating around your town by understanding the road signs, or getting into a taxi and telling the driver where you want to go, without having to resort to sign language.

On a deeper level, it doesn't matter how many books you read, I don't believe that you can truly become part of a community, or get to know its identity and eccentricities, or its history and customs, until you speak the language. There are some things I can't even describe in English because a different language will describe it more succinctly, eloquently and delicately. Our family has been known to adopt these phrases and mix them in with English. We do this when we move to a new country, so we can speak in code in front of the children - it's amazing how quickly they learn and pick up on things when they want to!

My children have all just accepted that English is just one way to communicate, because they have been exposed to different languages from a very young age. It is completely normal to them and they don't look at foreign speakers strangely, but seem to be able to mimic many different accents really quickly.

When my parents were visiting us in Argentina they looked after our two youngest children, while we enjoyed a wonderful trip to Peru. Our three-year-old instinctively interpreted between my parents and our 'empleada' (domestic help), who spoke no English. All of our children are very good at helping others when they are struggling to communicate. I love the fact that they will just have a go at speaking a few words of the language of the country we are visiting, whether it is Brazilian Portuguese, French, German or Arabic. I have never seen them embarrassed to do so. They have leant that "please", "thank you", "hello" and "goodbye" in any language will get them a long way, or perhaps an extra scoop of ice cream in a restaurant, from a charmed waiter or waitress!

Adults tend to be more reluctant, and self-conscious, but mistakes just become funny stories. When living in Serbia it was very common for friendly and well-meaning older ladies to pat our son's head or pinch his cheeks. He didn't take kindly to such attention and quickly learned to say 'ne' (no) repeatedly to try to deflect their advances. When we went on holiday to Greece, he had a similar effect on Greek ladies. He expressed his annoyance with the familiar 'ne'. Unfortunately for him, 'ne' means 'yes' in Greek!

What other expats have to say

Wendy, a Brit who lived in the US

I loved working in the USA, but they do expect you to talk like the Queen. I found myself having a better British accent when I worked there than I did at home. I naturally spoke there in a way they expected me to - far posher! If they'd heard my normal accent, they'd have been quite disappointed!

Adrian, a Brit who has lived in Albania, Croatia, Bosnia, Greece

I've made lots of language mistakes; in Greek for example, telling a lady that there were lots of cauliflowers flying around in the room instead of using the correct Greek word for mosquitos.
My wife learned Albanian, Greek, Croatian, Turkish, Bulgarian and Pomak. I learned enough to get by in some of those languages.

Imogen, a Brit who has lived in Hong Kong, Singapore, Sri Lanka, Kenya, Australia

On my first visit to London, as a five-year-old, our parents took us to McDonald's in Baker Street. Being a chatty person, I turned to the man on the table next to me - a proper Cockney - and said: "Do you speak English?"
He replied: "Of course I do, love. What do you think I speak, Swahili?" To which the rather precocious me replied, "I do". "Go on then", came the baffled reply...."Jumbo, Habari, Masuri....", I rattled off. Unsurprisingly, he responded to with: "Cor blimey". We were in the process of moving from Kenya to Hong Kong at the time.

Norma, a Brit living in France

My eight-year-old son failed to come home from French school one day. I was distraught as neither he nor I could speak French fluently at that point. When he did come home, I found out I had misunderstood that his class had been on a day trip! Big red face for me!

Lori, a Kenyan living in Singapore

I have lots of funny stories based on language problems.
Supermarket lady: "You need to pay $2 for the childrens".
Me: "Why?"
Supermarket lady: "Because it's the childrens, and you have to."
Me: "I don't think I have to. I can choose to, but I don't have to."
Supermarket lady: "Yes you do! You get the childrens from the fridge, you have to pay more."
Me: "Ohhhh!!!! The chilled drinks.... Ok, here's more money."

Elizabeth, a Brit, who lived in Japan and now Belgium

When visiting a noodle bar in Japan in the summer it is usual to have cold noodles. I asked the waiter, in very limited Japanese, if they could be hot using the Japanese a word for hot "Atsui". He thought I meant my already cold noodles were not cold enough so presented them back to me on a plate of ice. Needless to say, I just had to eat them ... yum?!

Anon, a Brit living in Spain
Once I ordered a polla sandwich in a Spanish cafe rather than a sandwich de pollo. I'll let you find the translation for that one!

Claudia, a German who has lived in Switzerland, the US and the Netherlands
We parked the car at the airport in Zürich. A lady came up and asked us something in Swiss German. My husband answered in high German. She did not understand. I tried to tell her in German, but she did not get it. So, we switched into English: and suddenly it was not a problem anymore. She understood where to go to find what she was looking for.

Kate, a Brit living in Denmark
I cried in the middle of the supermarket in our first month here as I couldn't work out how to collect the nappies I had ordered online from an automated collection machine. It seemed like such a simple thing to do but so difficult at the time!

Where do you start?

Here are Amy's top tips:
- Prioritise getting a good language teacher very early on. If you are seen to be making an effort, no matter how dreadful your command of the language, then locals will be far more likely to try to help you or meet you more than halfway. If you make no effort there will always be a considerable gap between you and the community you are living in;

- Never arrive in a country without knowing how to greet the officer at passport control or thank them as you move on;

- Don't start with the grammar or the small talk. Prioritise what you need most urgently in day-to-day life, for example, the names of fruits, vegetables, meats and basic groceries if you are in a country where supermarkets aren't so good. You'll also probably need to know how to ask someone to repeat something more slowly so that you can understand;

- Learn numbers quickly! You will avoid the bitter taste of working out that you have been ripped off by (rare) unscrupulous shopkeepers. Make sure you know your address and telephone number too.

Work

Sometimes the decision-making process for moving abroad is simple. You are offered a job that is interesting and pays the bills, and gives you a chance to live in a new and exciting place[19].

When you're part of a family unit the thought process is somewhat different:

- You are offered a job that is interesting and pays the bills; your partner feels torn as they will have to give up their career, while giving you the opportunity to further yours.;

- Your partner feels torn as they will have to leave family and friends and find a new support network;

- You are unsure of how the children will cope with a new language and making new friends;

- You worry about your aging parents, etc., etc.,

The web of complications can be so elaborate you begin to wish you hadn't been offered the job in the first place.

On a personal level, the choice to live overseas is often boils down to a financial one. Nearly, 63% of people think they are better off

---

[19] Expat Explorers' survey: 25% of respondents moved abroad with their jobs; 54% moved aboard with their partner's job; 21% moved with parents or independently. Most people (66%) move abroad for improved work opportunities. The three biggest single sectors promoting global mobilisation are the financial services (15%), oil and gas (11%) and professional services (8%). Aviation, manufacturing, education, construction and hospitality also feature highly.

financially as expats[20]. For corporates, governments and charities, the role of the expat is becoming more integral in supporting their labour requirements. This has led to several interesting trends and issues for both parties:

- For employers, increasing awareness of cost sensitivities has meant expat packages are not as generous as they used to be. They were often used to tempt foreign skilled workers by covering school fees, health care and moving costs;

- For employees, there is growing financial pressure. It is increasingly common for both people in a couple have to work full time to make ends meet. For some, this means a growing reluctance to accept positions abroad, particularly when there is no compensation to cover the loss of a second wage;

- Developing technology and globalisation has created commuter expats, who are based in their home country but spend a significant amount of time abroad. Although the family isn't required to move, a huge pressure is put on family life, relationships and the spouse who remains at home;

- Free movement of labour can still create exciting opportunities for those who haven't put down roots, and are looking for a new cultural experience. Positions can be short-lived or contract based.

Believe it or not, if you are moving country with your job, you're the lucky one. Your partner isn't necessarily going to come along for the ride just to sip cocktails. The tangle of emotions they experience

---

[20] Expat Explorers' survey: 14% thought they were financially disadvantaged and 24% were not sure. Just over a quarter stated that being financially better off as the top advantage of being an expat, ranking it second in a list. Cultural experience topped the list with 32% of the vote.

is much more complex.

Let's start with the term that people either love or hate: *the trailing spouse*. To some this offers an explanation for all that they have had to give up to move. They realise that they are gaining new and exciting experiences, but they want recognition for how much of a change they have had to make. Some might feel like a victim, or the hard done by member of the family. Not only have they given up their job, in favour of yours, but their career path has now been interrupted, while yours scampers on.

Others are more positive. They go to extreme lengths not to be seen as a victim. They want to be seen as an enabler, holding the power in their hands, squeezing every ounce of opportunity out of the situation.

Regardless of whether you feel like an enabler, or a trailing spouse, most people just want someone to say thank you. People rarely do. While your partner is at work and the children are at school, you're getting to grips with where to shop for food, who to call in emergencies, how to communicate with locals without using hand signals that may be rude, how to sort out a social life - sometimes with a toddler or baby in tow.

These tasks will probably still pass to you even if you decide you can go back to work. As far as everyone else is concerned, it's rarely essential to go back to work straight away. Settling in takes priority.

When we moved to the US, I was unable to work for a while, due to visa restrictions. I was carving out a resemblance of a social life, through a mothers and toddlers group, but I didn't want baby vomit to be all I had in common with my friends. So, I went back to college. Not only did this allow me to meet new people with similar interests, but it helped to plug any emerging career gap that might creep onto my CV.

When we moved to the UAE, I decided to investigate the daunting world of getting a trade licence so I could start some consulting work. I did the same when I moved to Singapore, and set up my business a third time when I moved back to the UK. I could definitely tick the box that said I had worked abroad.

There are plenty of books that address the international career move. There are few that look at creating your own career to fit in with the current circumstances. I found I could network and find work, once I had conducted some market research and identified my niche. I found it hard, however, to develop a strategy that coped with moving country repeatedly. Basically, despite best efforts to take clients with me, contracts soon fizzled out and I was left building my business from scratch again. This wasn't a hobby job. I needed to develop a convincing narrative to show how the fragmented elements of my business indicated success, if I was to have employment options in the future. Luckily, the term 'portfolio career', has become en vogue, enabling me to weave a common thread through my journalism, corporate communications, travel and interior design interests.

Entrepreneurial operations and business building doesn't suit everyone. Unfortunately, depending where you are, there are few career jobs open to expats. Even if you're lucky enough to find one, eventually either you or your partner will inevitably be offered another role in another country. You'll have to face the same dilemma as when you first moved - who puts their career on hold to move to pastures new?

Meet Allison

Allison, a Canadian, moved to the UAE with her husband's job, temporarily putting her career, as a learning and development professional, on hold to do so.

The opportunity to live abroad came at the right time and it wasn't a difficult decision to make. I was winding down my job in Canada and so didn't start looking for the next contract.

As a couple, we talked about the move, but the decision was quite easy as we had previously thought about living abroad. I was up for the adventure. I had some degree of control and influence in the initial stages of leaving. We toured houses and schools together, so made big decisions together.

My husband moved to Dubai three months before me, so I wrapped up everything in Canada, sold the house, packed up, and organised plans for the summer.

When the family was reunited, I didn't have to rush into getting a job. It meant I was able to take six months to put the family first, acclimatise and settle in a new country.

One of the biggest changes for me, was that I had to suspend my Western values of equality and fairness. Human rights were very different in Dubai. Being Jewish and from North America meant that I didn't have a community to link to. I wasn't particularly observant of my faith, but I was very aware of the wider region's history. Being of Jewish faith wasn't facilitated or supported in any way, so I felt the differences more keenly.

These values were also put to the test in the work arena, where women are in the minority, and women's rights are questionable. This was completely at odds with my professional focus of helping to improve individual and team performance.

I found contract work through a friend, another mother at school, in the learning and development sector, working with a training company.

There's plenty of red tape to get tangled in, but the waters were quite muddy as to how trade licences operated. The company made it simple by paying me in cash, but it was legal and above board, so that's all that mattered.

The decision to go back to work wasn't about career progression. Looking back, I think I was depressed. The kids were at school and I would often spend my day watching reruns on TV. I wasn't aware of feeling depressed. I thought I was bored - I was lonely. That said, there were invites from friends, but I got into a habit of isolating myself.

When I made the commitment to go back to work, I had somewhere to be, and a responsibility to people outside of my family. I have a high degree of professional integrity, so I wanted to do the job well, which helped to drive me and give me purpose. It doesn't suit me, or my mental health, to be at home, wholly focussed on the kids.

It's not necessarily difficult to find a job, although that obviously depends on your location, but you do need to be open to doing things a different way. You might need to be more entrepreneurial, or change your working hours, or even your sector.

I found there was a different level of accountability, and a different definition of what made a quality product, from what I was used to. The company I worked for was very focussed on sales. They were good at getting business but less concerned with delivering a high-quality outcome. In general, I found the bar was low for quality of business in my industry. I, personally, might have been working in a mediocre way, but I was one of their top-rated facilitators.

It's difficult to know how these differences come about. It could be that in a transient community you don't always have the right balance of skills. Or it could have more to do with culture and local working practices. The clients don't have high expectations. The relationships were all very transactional. It was about tactics rather strategy.

One of the best jobs I had was conducting some professional training for Emirati women through the local university. I felt like I was contributing to women's liberation in a country where women are not equal to men. The course delegates used to like it when I'd try and speak Arabic, and they would try and teach me phrases. It was such a great experience. Many of my students were married, young women who were choosing to work for the first time. They were curious and engaged. It's great when you feel like you're making a difference.

I would share photos with them from home in Canada. One particular picture was of a sunny, spring day, but the person in the photo was still wearing boots and a down-filled vest, and there was snow on the ground. They couldn't believe that we called these conditions "spring". It can be very exciting and rewarding to share information and insights into your background, in a reciprocal way.

Women are good at using their skills creatively. That said, there weren't many female expats who had careers. They had jobs just to keep busy and mentally active. Men were the ones with careers and professions. There's a lot of juggling between domestic life, family and work. It doesn't suit everyone. Lots of women channelled that capability into volunteering and helping at school.

As we had moved country with my husband's job, it was a bit of a compromise for me. My career advancement was limited in favour of seeing another part of the world. I have no regrets. You need to be mindful of the trade-off and be happy with it. I made an intentional choice: I gained life experience, a greater appreciation of diversity, and met some brilliant people.

What other expats have to say

Fiona, a Brit living in the US

Living in the USA has been generally a wonderful experience with plenty of travel and adventure. From a career perspective it has not been great though. I finally have a green card and can work again, but I feel intimidated and lacking in up to date skills. On the plus side, not being able to work for money led me to explore other avenues and I got to be a volunteer call screener for National Public Radio and became a broadcaster on a small local radio station. Now I am easing my way back into paid employment by running an Airbnb, which is great fun. My advice would be, if you can't work because of visa restrictions, get a volunteer job.

Angie, an American living in the UK

I guess ideally you need to have a "reason" to get out and integrate into the new community as soon as possible, whether that's a job, or a volunteer role, or a course. I found it difficult because I was working on a business based in the US, before I had UK work authorisation. The upside was I could be in the UK with my partner, but it was pretty isolating working from home in a new country and that was really hard.

Anon, an American living in Australia

I think we would have settled quicker if my wife and I had been better mentally prepared. I had a job and I started right away so it was a bit easier for me, but my wife had to spend the first few months finding work. Being able to realise "I'm sad, or lonely, or whatever...but this is normal" would have been a good framework to have.

Anon, an Australian living in Singapore

I find that a lot of trailing spouses are in my position where we are unable to work, so therefore [I have] more time to socialise.

Where do you start?

- Recognise you're starting your job search from a different position and reset your mental model. Allison observed that when you're looking for work in your home market you have existing relationships and you know where to go to start conversations. There are a lot of resources to help. Moving to a new country you almost need to know someone who knows someone. It's a short cut to understanding the system. It's difficult to get running from a standing start. She said: "Just knowing this helped me to understand that the process wasn't difficult, just different."

- If financially possible, give yourself six months to settle in, build your network and find out how your new country ticks.

- Do your research. Find out about your new market and the red tape that surrounds it.

- Do something completely new. Brainstorm all the jobs you ever wanted to do. What did the 17-year-old you dream of becoming? If you're not trained to do paid work, you may be able to volunteer or do an internship.

Technology

At the age of seven, in the early 1980s, I moved to Kuwait with my family. We didn't have a telephone. There wasn't a door-to-door postal system. Forget any new-fangled fairies that magically carried messages through the ether. What we did have was a tape recorder. It even had unnecessary chrome panels to indicate that it was state of the art technology.

Every couple of months, my siblings and I were asked to perform for the tape. We had quite a repertoire of nursery rhymes and songs, so we were happy to oblige.

This frivolity was usually followed by serious adult business, which involved a lot of talking about how we were, what we were doing and that we missed everyone.

It was customary for my mother to bar us from the flat as she recorded her message home, trying to sound as natural as possible, while feeling terribly self-conscious.

The tape was then duly sent by sea to reach its destination months down the line.

Three decades later, I moved from the UK to the US with a baby and a toddler. The wide-open plains of Chicago were bewildering to me. I didn't recognise the shops brands and I didn't know the landmarks, so navigation was a huge issue.

It was then that I realised how different my expat experience was from my parents', just because of technology. My lifesaver, and my connection to the outside world, came along in the form of an iPhone (other products are available). Technology helped me to find my feet. Internet access on the go meant I had access to maps, and more importantly a little blue dot telling me where I was. I would never be lost again. I was able to shop online, check out reviews, book restaurants and cinema reservations. Most importantly I was able to call home, for free.

I was also able to join local groups virtually. This was no substitute to meeting people in person, but it was a comforting step forwards, rather than a giant leap of faith.

Before I left home, I hated social networking sites. I didn't have a particular need to know what people had for breakfast, or the minutiae of everyday life. I became a fan, however. Social networking has shrunk our world so we can keep in touch with friends and family all over the world. Of course, it can be trite and superficial (even alarming or dangerous), but I found it a great way of gaining a little insight into how people were doing, making face to face conversations easier when you've been apart for a long time.

One observation is the speed with which we got broadband and mobile phones set up with each move. In the US it took weeks to get ourselves connected. By the fourth move, back to the UK, having transitioned through the UAE and Singapore, it was done in days if not hours. In part, this is because of improved customer service. However, we were also starting to get to grips with the process much quicker, by asking the right questions and honing our requirements.

Dependency on technology is not a good thing, however. As a consultant, I've had to set up my business in each country I've lived in. In some places the broadband speed has been like lighting. In others it's a matter of crossing fingers and hoping there won't be a power cut before you've managed to email your client the report you promised by the end of the day.

It's not just the less developed countries that suffer these problems. I currently live in the last road on the outskirts of a village in England. It's semi-rural, but not remote. There is no such thing as fibre broadband to the house, which frustratingly stops at the end of the road. Internet speeds can be so slow I'm thinking of reverting to the trusty tape recorder, chrome and all.

Meet Justin

Justin, a Brit living in Singapore, admits being slow on the technology take up, but found it made expat life easier.

I was always a bit of a dinosaur when it came to technology, but soon realised just how much benefit it offered in terms of connectivity as well as cost-savings. I still remember being told off by my parents for the long and expensive transatlantic calls I used to make to my best friend in the States on our birthdays and other special occasions. Now an email or a message on their Facebook page is all it takes, although it's not as personal, I admit.

It's only recently that I've upgraded to an iPhone. I'm now playing catch-up realising just how technology can improve my life. I love making movies of my sons playing sports to send to relatives. I no longer have the need for a video camera, camera, satnav or MP3 player. Everything I need is one phone. Some people realised that years ago! There are also plenty of new technologies on the way, which will make connectivity even easier. Soon virtual and augmented reality may even make it feel like you are there in the room with your family.

I haven't had an easy relationship with social media, however. I have never been a fan of Facebook and enjoyed a five-year hiatus when I terminated my account. I didn't like the constant stream of carefully curated photos from people bragging and showing how amazing their lives were. Most were friends of friends or old-school buddies I had lost touch with. I viewed it as a form of entertainment not really a social platform. Recently I decided to re-activate my account and now only have a small and exclusive group of family and friends as my connections. This allows me to keep up to date with them, send real-time messages and post up pictures of my two sons growing up. If you control and manage technology and social media how you want, then it can work for you. Otherwise, it is an addictive waste of time. Facetime is a very useful and personal way to stay in touch with friends and relatives when living overseas. I am also an active LinkedIn user and am amazed at how people find me from the other side of the world with work assignment offers.

When I was growing up in London, my best friend moved to California. We would send each other airmail letters that took at least two weeks to arrive. It was hard to stay in touch when our lives were moving at such a fast pace. Now it's so easy to keep in touch via email, WhatsApp and Facebook. Technology has changed my life for the better, especially as an expat with strong connections back to the UK. Of course, it is not as good as being with your loved ones in person. A Christmas Skype call is great but it can make you feel homesick, wishing you were sitting at the table about to tuck into roast turkey and the trimmings with your family. I guess you can't have it all as an expat!

What other expats have to say

Tory, a Brit living in South Africa

I moved for the first time when I was 13-years-old. We had to write letters to our friends and then wait six weeks for a reply! Nowadays, my kids can FaceTime their friends across the world in live time...the world is changing so fast.

The first three months are the time to get out and meet as many people as possible. The world is a very small place - with social media/Facetime you are never that far away from anyone, regardless of the country they or you live in.

Anon, an Australian, who had lived in Indonesia, Iran and Doha

I found it funny how far technology had grown in my home country coming back. The looks I would get from shop assistants when I didn't know what they were talking about when they said: "Do you want to tap it?" for payment. The first time, I replied: "Tap what?" all sorts of thoughts going through my head!

They thought I was from another planet. I had a giggle to myself and have had lots of giggles since moving back. You sometimes just have to laugh it off.

Anon, from Australia, has live in Ireland, Japan and UK

Keep in touch with friends you left behind or have moved on - technology is your saviour.

Kate, a Brit living in Denmark

Find expat groups via Facebook, put yourself out there and go to as many events as you can to get started and meet people. Be the person who makes the suggestion about meeting up for coffee or dinner or play dates. Others will be thinking about it, but someone has to make the first move. All this was way out of my comfort zone, but you have to do it to meet people. I guess it's a bit like dating!

Where do you start?

- Sorting out your phone and broadband when you move to a new country is always at the top of the to-do list. How you go about it differs from country to country. Do your research before you go, for example choosing your providers, so you can hit the ground running.

- Focus on making a fast decision on suppliers rather than spending weeks doing research and losing sight of the aim: get connected to start talking. The decision doesn't need to be perfect just good enough to get you started. Consider shorter contracts, that you can get out of more quickly, to buy you time.

- Make technology work for you. Create closed group chats for your family, so you can stay in contact with a quick hello. Make sure you're not a slave to technology though. If you spend too long looking at Facebook feeds you may start to feel homesick. Keep control by using it as a tool to help you keep in contact, rather than a way friends can show you what you're missing.

- Following your favourite television programmes is easier with streaming services such as Netflix. Staying in contact with friends and family is easier with Skype and WhatsApp. However, there may be restrictions or limitations in the country you're moving to. Investigate some local Facebook groups so you can ask advice.

- Use streaming radio to give you a link to home. In Dubai and Singapore, we 'time shifted' the previous day's breakfast show from the UK as our morning soundtrack. The weather was irrelevant, and traffic advice unhelpful, but it gave us a small sense of continuity and connection.

Health

"We need a paediatrician," is the first thing I heard as a new mother. A sentence that fills every vein and capillary surging with adrenaline and dread.

My daughter was born with a very rare, life threatening condition, and at 13-months-old had to undergo a gruelling seven-hour operation on her skull.

So why, with a toddler, who had had such a stressful start in life, and a new baby, would we decide to move abroad?

There are so many ways to answer this question. It was a fantastic opportunity. We love to travel. We love to learn about new cultures. We wanted our daughters to understand the world they live in too, and their place in it.

It wasn't an easy decision though. If my husband had come home from work to tell me we were being sent to deepest Africa or Outer Mongolia moving abroad would not have been an option. Chicago, however, presented itself as a relatively safe destination, with good healthcare specialists who understood our daughter's condition. Work was also accommodating of our need to return to the UK a couple of times a year to see our neurosurgeon.

When I explain my daughter's condition to friends, and her fighting start to life, the first thing people always say is: "I don't know how you coped with that." Obviously, you do because there is no option, and the human brain cleverly numbs emotions so you can put one foot in front of the other. That's all you have to do: put one foot in front of the other and keep going.

This helped make our decision to jump into expat life a little easier. There were so many benefits, and as long as the children's lives were not in danger, it was an opportunity we wanted to grasp with both hands. When it comes to moving to a new country, you can't dip your toe in the water and see how you feel. You have to pack up every element of your life and commit to moving. In seven years, we've moved four times, and now aged nine and eleven, the girls are well-adjusted, streetwise, culturally accepting and inspired. They are excited that there is an entire globe they can continue to explore.

It wasn't all plain sailing. We were no longer entitled to free-at-delivery British healthcare so had to rearrange to see our specialists in the private sector. The content of our private health insurance package had to be scrutinised, challenged and negotiated, as without the right level of care, our international move wouldn't have happened.

I had to accept greater responsibility for, and understanding of, the type of care my daughter required too, taking on the lynchpin role of project managing her healthcare. I had to research the right specialists, fight health insurers to ensure they delivered, and manage cashflow and piles of bills. I also had to learn how health insurance worked in different countries. In the States, all bills were sent directly to our insurer and I had choice in the specialists we saw. In Singapore, it was a different story. I had to pay and claim back thousands of pounds' worth of healthcare, without full confidence that the bill would ever be paid. The complicated nature of insurance policies means the provider always has a loophole, even if you're sure you have the right cover.

Keeping tabs on the claims and corresponding payments, when random amounts appeared in my bank account, was a complete nightmare, which used to take up hours of my time. I expected different insurance companies to have different processes, but this was even the case when we moved to a new country with the same insurer.

It was emotionally draining too. In our seven years overseas, no-one from an insurance company ever talked to me with compassion, understanding the stress of looking after a child with a life-threatening condition. I was just a transaction.

Despite the endless phone calls and emails to chase payments, the research to find the right support and the problematic nature of international healthcare, once we could make an informed decision, life abroad was still an option we wanted to realise. We had our eyes open and put one foot in front of the other. Everything is possible.

Meet Bec

Moving abroad is a huge step particularly because you're leaping into the unknown. Healthcare is one of the major concerns new expats face, and of course standards vary all around the world. You need to feel confident that your day to day medical needs are met as well as any emergencies. Health, however, is always changing. You may go aboard in tip-top condition, but what happens when you discover a concern?

Bec is originally from Ireland, but has lived in Malawi, Australia (where she met her husband), Singapore and the Netherlands. She faced an extremely traumatic experience. While most expats won't go through these extremes, they do at some point face the logistical and financial difficulties of dealing with complex healthcare.

Growing up as an expat in Africa, we always had top level international health cover - we grew up in a place where you really didn't want to have to go to hospital, so our policy included worldwide coverage.

With a brother and two sisters, we had the usual childhood bumps and scratches. Supported by good health insurance, we had claims for accidents, some requiring ongoing care. My brother even ended up having a pretty major back operation in his late teens that had to be done in Dublin.

I am sure the policy underwriter ended up unemployed - over the years they must have paid out way more than my father's work contract could possibly have contributed.

When I moved to Australia, I kept the same insurance and benefited from continuation of coverage, so when I converted to local cover they waived the waiting periods. I had top level private insurance and again, that poor underwriter didn't get off any easier: I had two caesarian section births, a couple of minor operations, skin checks, glasses... You name it, if I was eligible for it, I availed myself of it.

In 2011, we moved to Singapore with two small kids, and immediately faced a different kind of difficulty. Top level international insurance for the family was going to be very, very expensive. The job we moved with was on a 'local' package, rather than an expat package so it didn't include any financial contribution towards housing, schools or - more importantly - international health cover. Unlike my experience as a child, we were moving to a place that was renowned for its high-quality healthcare, and we were confident that should any major health issues beset us, we would be well looked after. We decided to take out top level private healthcare cover for Singapore only, although this was against friends' advice. One school mum had to take her son to Switzerland to receive experimental treatment, "otherwise he would have certainly died". It was probably fully covered under their international health insurance.

It was a real dilemma for us, but who can predict the future? We certainly didn't have enough spare cash to insure the whole family with a decent level of international care. We had some support for outpatient costs from my husband's company and basic hospitalisation cover. We were confident that if anything dire was to happen, we couldn't be in a better place.

Then, our middle child was diagnosed with a heart murmur at three and a half. We had a referral to a local paediatric cardiologist, and so I took my overexcited daughter to see an underwhelming dour man who poked and prodded, and attempted an ECG. He then declared that she needed an MRI immediately and almost certainly surgery without delay. He even started discussing surgery costs right there and then!

It was such a serious situation we sought a second professional opinion, and were told by our Aussie paediatrician that she could refer us to someone in Sydney, since we were about to go there on holiday. We attended the Children's Hospital at Westmead, and after a more successful ECG, the cardiologist concurred with the Singaporean doctor but recommended a vastly different course of action.

We were told that, yes, she had a structural problem with her aorta, and it would have to be surgically corrected, but it was better to wait until she had grown a little. We had annual reviews that we planned around visits home and our daughter continued to grow normally and thrive. When she reached seven years old, they recommended more scans as there was now a blood pressure differential between her lower and upper body, evidence that perhaps her heart wasn't pumping the blood around her body as efficiently as it should. A CT scan revealed the full extent of the problem and surgery was planned for a few months later.

At this stage, we battled with the decision of whether to pay up ourselves or to have the surgery in Singapore, and hopefully have it covered by our insurance. Then we hit a couple of snags. Firstly, if it was a congenital issue our Singapore insurance may not cover us; secondly, if we had the surgery in Singapore it would certainly cost upwards of £100,000; thirdly, we couldn't get a recommendation for a surgeon that could perform the required surgery with confidence. All in all, we opted to go ahead with the surgery in Sydney knowing that we didn't qualify for Australian Medicare, as we had been away too long, and that we would be liable for all costs. We were in a fortunate position in that we had been saving for a house and since we didn't own property, we had some funds available. In addition, a very generous family member contributed some money as a gift.

We worked out the timing for the surgery, so my mother flew in from Dublin, to mind our other two children, while my husband and I took our daughter to Sydney. We had a week before the surgery with my in-laws, and suffice it to say, it wasn't an easy time for anyone.

The surgery itself took 10 hours and even a year on, it brings me to tears to recall the day. Health and youth were on her side though. Our daughter was in fine health going into the surgery and bounced back and was discharged after two nights in intensive care and two nights on the ward. She underwent open heart surgery to basically reconstruct her aorta by creating a web of collateral vessels, which all combined to create sufficient blood flow for her body. The main artery had twisted back on itself twice and was, to all intents and purposes, impossible. By waiting a few extra years, the surgeon was able to create an aorta by inserting a special tube that was of sufficient diameter to support her growth through her teens and hopefully into early adulthood.

However, there was a secondary problem. The new tube created a compression and six months later she had the adjacent pulmonary artery stented. This was a minor procedure in comparison though.

All in all, our stay in Sydney lasted eight weeks. A week after our return to Singapore she was back at squad training with her school swimming team. It has been a year, two months and six days since her operation - not that I'm counting or anything. She has been in great physical health, although the whole ordeal has left us all with an aversion to hospitals.

Financially, we worked out that if we had paid for the private health insurance we would still be 'in the money' by a few thousand dollars, but it was never about the cost. It was about making the right medical decision balanced with ensuring we had the funds to give our daughter the right care. We have since moved to the Netherlands, and this time, the first thing we asked for was full, top level international health insurance. We're not risking a second bite of that cherry.

What other expats have to say

Melinda, an American, who has lived in Singapore and Hong Kong
I had an attorney go through my employment contract so that things like retirement pay, health insurance, and repatriation were addressed more appropriately.

Becker, a Brit, who has lived in Brunei and Saudi Arabia
I think children benefit from expat life, especially the better schooling and health care.

Amy, who has lived in Ghana and the UAE
Consider your move very carefully. Think about all aspects of life. Don't underestimate social cohesion, your own culture, the quality of education and healthcare, and your own personal values and needs.

Petra, who has lived in Russia, Argentina and France
We found there was a disparity between standard childhood vaccinations schedules in each country we've lived in. It's worth being aware of this so you can make informed decisions.

Where do you start?

- If you've been given healthcare insurance as part of your employment package check it covers everything you need it to. Be prepared to negotiate. Many policies don't cover pre-existing or congenital conditions.

- Ask neighbours, work colleagues, or contacts from local community groups on Facebook, for recommendations for good healthcare professionals, including paediatricians, dentists, general practitioners and Accident & Emergency departments.

- When you're happy with your healthcare providers keep a list on the fridge door, family noticeboard or somewhere everyone can see. The last thing you need in an emergency is to scrabble around trying to find a phone number.

The role of women

I first moved abroad as an adult with a toddler tucked under one arm and a baby under the other. We moved from the leafy, rural British countryside to the suburban Mid-West of the United States, an area where I had no family, no friends and no support network.

At first, everything was exciting and new. I was kept busy learning about my new surroundings, looking after the children and setting up home; too busy to think. However, over time, I began to feel confused about who I was and where I was going. I just didn't feel like me. Some may put this down to baby blues, but it was more than that.

I started to feel overpowered by negative feelings and a lack of direction – I had always wanted to travel and live abroad, but I had been uprooted at a time when I didn't feel I had any control. I had a brain that I wanted to use, but I spent all day clapping with a three-year-old, and wiping sticky substances off surfaces. I felt like a victim of circumstances, rather than an empowered young woman who was making things happen. I was questioning my identity and how I fitted into this new landscape. I was the same person, I just needed to adapt.

I made huge efforts to meet new people by joining a local toddler group. People were very friendly, but found it hard to relate to me. I couldn't blame them as I was finding it hard to relate to me. I no longer had my career as an indicator of who I was. Of course, the same would have been true if I'd remained in the UK. The difference was that I wasn't cossetted by a recognisable structure – there was no framework or foundation upon which to build. I just felt like I was trying to wade in thick mud, constantly having to make an effort, but getting nowhere fast.

In what I realised was a common experience for trailing spouses, my husband was able to settle much more quickly. He went to work and interacted with colleagues in the same way he had done in the UK. My children settled quickly because I was with them, and I was their recognisable structure. When they were older, their structure revolved around school.

The big question was "why do I feel so strange and out of place?" When people asked: "What do you do?" I felt obliged to caveat my answer. I'd say: "I look after my two young children at the moment, but I used to be …." It's a shame really, as the role of stay-at-home mother is the hardest in the world, and you don't get any training. It's just society could better relate to me if they knew intellectually what I did. A job title is often a shortcut to assessing someone's interests, social standing and education level.

What I hadn't realised was that I was making my life harder because I hadn't *created* my identity.

Then came the turning point. Many expats feel a dip, usually after six months, which often manifests itself as an intense feeling of homesickness[21]. I began to understand that this dip wasn't a sign that I preferred to be in my home country. It was a sign that I had worked hard, hanging on to the rollercoaster as it pelted around the learning curve, and I was coming up to an opportunity watershed. The partner at home, or the trailing spouse, has more choices, more facets of life to deal with, from finding a supermarket and

---

[21] Expat Explorers' survey: The three top disadvantages of expat life are being away from friends and family (57%), the physical distance from home (21%) and legal restrictions (10%). It takes most people between six and 12 months to feel settled (31%); 19% took between three and six months; For 23% the process took more than a year. Some people (6%) never feel settled. This can contribute to expats returning home early, or unhappiness if they stay.

fathoming out how to use public transport, to plunging into the world of work or study. For some, this is daunting. For others, it's an exciting range of possibilities.

The wood had been in the way of the trees. Feeling overwhelmed and over-stimulated in a new environment is inevitable. The key is to accept the situation, ride the storm, take stock and choose a direction. So, I worked out how to get around without getting lost; I looked at day care options for the children to give me the support I missed from home; I sussed out the social nuances and began to learn how people interacted and operated in my newly adopted culture.

It wasn't plain sailing, but I was able to start assessing situations and options, rather than just reacting to them. I realised that the many sides of my identity didn't mean I was fragmented. It meant I was able to reframe and work in different ways with different people. I may not have initially recognised who I was in this new land, but then it was a unique set of circumstances. I wasn't necessarily reinventing myself, although that was entirely possible. I was developing different parts of my life. I could redesign my décor, create a supportive environment for my family, go back to college, take up a new hobby, get a job or network and freelance.

It's empowering when you realise you haven't lost your identity, but have the chance to develop it. Sometimes we don't know how robust we can be, especially when we feel like a victim of circumstance.

To borrow some words from a grand dame of my new home, Eleanor Roosevelt: "A woman is like a tea bag – you can't tell how strong she is until you put her in hot water."

Meet Angie

Angie, an American living in the UK, didn't have a traditional expat experience. She moved to the UK to be with her British boyfriend and ended up staying.

It took me a long time to settle into British life, even with a British boyfriend to support me, and that took me by surprise. We met at a US business school and graduated feeling that the world was our oyster. He moved back to the UK for a work opportunity, so at the time it wasn't a huge decision for me to move too as I had a more adaptable job, running my own business.

I was possibly a bit naïve as I didn't think about how it would work on a practical level. I probably thought we could work six months in each country. We got married and kids came along. You obviously can't live very easily in two places then.

Initially, the settling process was very difficult. I worked by myself at home, as my company was based in the US, talking to people I never met in person. There were relatively few chances for local social interaction, so I didn't make local friends. My husband would come home from work, and I'd ask to hear about his meetings, and who he'd met.

I don't think I was able to settle fully, and finally feel grounded, until I worked full time in a UK office. It wasn't about being indoctrinated into the UK culture. It was more about being out in the world, instead of working from home and seeing the same four walls. I needed to find my professional identity, and develop some sort of social outreach. After all, I had worked my whole life, so it meant getting back on a corporate trajectory.

Having children in the UK, and joining baby groups, was a huge social stepping stone. I met some lovely people, and shared intense experiences with them, so we were connected emotionally. I found other people who didn't have family locally, and also needed the support.

It was a natural step to have children in the UK. We have a house, a job, the health system is really good and it's a good quality of life, so there was no real decision to make. The children have two passports and citizenship in both countries. That means that they have options and choices.

I always wanted to move back to the US at some point. My family are there, and I wanted to be geographically closer to them. We recently found ourselves in an awful situation. My mother is very ill, and I want to move back sooner than I had anticipated. It's a very stressful situation as we now have time pressures. The emotional stress and intensity is coming from me, not at all from my family. We don't know what will happen with my mother's health, but I don't want to regret not spending time with her. We don't have a job to move back with, or a home. We just know we need to move.

I've felt relatively settled in the UK, but I still feel a draw to the US, mainly because my family is there. There's a cultural element too. I won't ever fully belong in the UK. There are some things I'll never be able to relate to because I come from a different background, and can't access their world.

In conversations, there's sometimes an assumption that people have a shared experience. I'm never going to get what it is like to be a rower in Richmond with a flat in Mayfair. Of course, there are people I don't relate to in the US, but when you come from the same cultural background this creates shortcuts. You're more able to gauge whether you're going to rub along well with someone.

When you're new to an area, people can appear cliquey even if they are not. I'm aware that I'm always going to stand out as different as I have an American accent. People can still be lovely and friendly, but it can take longer to make lasting friendships as it isn't based on a common background or understanding. The biggest shock was when we started going to parties as a couple. People wouldn't talk to me, and I couldn't understand why. My husband explained a little about the traditional, formal side of British culture, where people wait to be introduced before chatting to strangers – they don't like to inconvenience others. It's bizarre and can make the British seems standoffish. I know they are not, but it was an important cultural lesson to learn.

I've learnt and understand a lot more than when I first moved here, but now I'm learning about the small details. I'll always be learning. The negative side might be that I sometimes feel on the community's edge. On the positive side, I have a diverse range of friendships with people from different nationalities and different walks of life. There is a great open mindedness here, and it's more of a cultural melting pot than where I was brought up in the US.

My environment might have an influence on my identity, but it's not massively important to me as long as there are frequent touch points with family at home. Maybe I'll always have a foot in both countries emotionally, even if it's not practical to actually live life that way.

What other expats have to say

Amy, an American living in Singapore

The idea of moving abroad is exotic and exciting. And when that wears off sometimes it can be difficult to continue adjusting. After six months and a new set of friends everything is much easier.

I had no idea I was struggling with the first move until we had been in Bangkok for eight months and my husband said: "You seem happy!" And I thought, "Really, was it that difficult that I wasn't happy?" Looking back, I really struggled at first but didn't know how much I had depended on him. I am really thankful for his patience, and for the friends that helped me find all the little things in my new country. It helped make all the difference.

Anon, a Belgium living in Singapore, who has also lived in the UK, Indonesia and France

Don't always expect understanding on the part of your partner's employers. I had to take care of the move on my own with two very young children as my husband had to attend "a very important" (just a regular) meeting on the day we moved in. He was then sent abroad for 10 days immediately afterwards.

I ended up wondering if I had been had. I was alone with two kids, not yet at school, traumatised, in an apartment twice as big as in my home country, with no helper, no dishwasher, and in the dark most of the time due to power problems. It turned out alright in the end though.

Where do you start?

- Take stock of what is important to you. How do you like to spend your free time? Finding time to do something you enjoy will help you settle. If you've always wanted to sketch, learn cake decorating, take up photography or write a book it could be a great way to meet like-minded people.

- If you're not working, seeing yourself as the enabler, rather than the victim of circumstance, can be a great help. Try writing a list of all the positive elements about your move. Now write a list of all the challenges. Challenge yourself each day, whether it's finding the supermarket or asking a new acquaintance for coffee.

- If you've moved country with your job, you may spend a lot of your free time socialising with colleagues. Try to extend your circle of friends. Perhaps organise a barbecue or evening drinks for neighbours, or join a special interest group.

Emotions

Missing family and friends is the biggest issue with expat life. On the positive side, moving abroad is the opportunity to live in a new country, culture and climate. On the flip side, you have to wave goodbye to loved ones. To make things worse, guilt is jogging besides you. Sometimes this guilt is so great it makes it impossible to feel settled. On average it takes people between six and 12 months to feel at home; some people (6%) never do[22].

It's easy for people left in your home country to think your life is gilded. Photographs always appear sunny, and as you're not in touch so often they aren't necessarily up to speed with your woes and worries. That doesn't mean there aren't any.

For most expats there are key elements they miss from home, and staying in contact with your homeland is part of the remedy. Every summer, the expat hubs around the world begin to shed foreigners who flood back to their homelands. Like birds, the migratory pattern is seasonal and routine.

We have lived in two of the world's biggest global expat hubs, Dubai and Singapore, and the phenomenon is similar in both places.

After school breaks up in June, families depart for the Western world, husbands or main breadwinners only staying a week or two at home before returning, alone, to their expat lives in order to eke out their annual leave.

---

[22] Expat Explorers Survey: It takes most people between six and 12 months to feel settled (31%); 19% took between three and six months; For 23% the process took more than a year. Some people (6%) never feel settled. This can contribute to expats returning home early, or unhappiness if they stay.

But why do we make this annual trip, at great expense and inconvenience? After all, the husband complains he misses the kids (and occasionally his wife), the children complain that they miss their toys and friends, and the wife is pulling her hair out carting children around single-handedly.

There are several reasons why the summer expat exodus is a necessary one.

- We're expats. We haven't emigrated. This means we still feel the pull of the homeland. We understand that circumstances and jobs change all the time, and while we may feel that we're here to stay, we could be gone tomorrow. We are part of a transient society.

- The homeland offers us stability in a global economic market that has had its ups and downs. We understand how the homeland ticks. We haven't had to learn its foibles, unlike our temporary expats homes. There is something comforting and effortless about that.

- Culture is important. What is the world without it? And so, we ensure our children know what they need to know about being British, or American, or Australian, or Kiwi.

- Family is really where the home is. We make fantastic friends in our expat homes, supporting each other with knowledge and a tissue when our mother is too far away. We all need support, and there is a certain magnetism about being with your own tribe.

- Friends also fit into the support category. We are the ones who have moved away, and we need to make every effort to stay in touch with homeland friends. Forget about them and you risk feeling like an expat when you return home, starting your network from scratch.

- And for some, the summer exodus is essential if we want to get out of the heat. Of course, we love the weather where we live, most of the time. But everyone needs a break from 50C heat and 99% humidity.

We all miss different things about our homeland. For some, it's a postal system that runs smoothly (Dubai doesn't have a door-to-door system). For others, it's the freedom of having a car (Singapore, where the cost is astronomical).

For me, apart from friends and family, it has been the British countryside, gastro pubs and historical houses. Oh, and strawberries that taste like strawberries, and don't cost $20 and have a guilt-inducing 10,000 air miles attached to them. All in all, emotions are more stable when you're in a land you understand.

Meet Josephine

How do you cope with the emotional tug when you're in a marriage of mixed nationalities and your homelands are in the different places? Does that make one of you an expat or are you an immigrant? Josephine, a Filipino who has lived in the UAE, Australia, Malaysia and Singapore, understands just how divided emotions can be.

I left the Philippines when I was 20 as I was offered a singing job in Melbourne.

My father wouldn't speak to me at first and it took us a while to be reconciled. You have to make a lot of sacrifices when you move abroad, especially when you move for work. It meant that I couldn't come home when I wanted, and even had to miss my grandmother's funeral. My father was so upset with me. He said: "When are you coming back? When I'm dead?"

I moved to Dubai, which is where I met my husband, who is British. I took him home to meet my family, and told them that we would hold the wedding in Dubai.

We returned home to make plans, and then I received the terrible news that one of my brothers had died of sepsis. I was singing on stage at a gig, and as soon as I stepped off the stage I received a call from home. I was in complete shock.

A couple of months later, my mother started getting ready to come over, and asked my father to get his passport ready. He said he wouldn't be needing it. He died of a stroke shortly before the wedding. It was as if he knew. It was a very sad time.

We moved to England a year ago and at first it was really tough, especially where I was living. I was the only Asian in a very white, middle class area.

People are very friendly, but it takes a while for everyone to figure out each other's culture.

The biggest issue for me is being so far away from my mother. She is now on her own, looking after another of my brothers, who has also suffered a stroke. It's such an expensive trip that we can't just pop over for short visits, and again your family is tied to work and school schedules.

My husband understands, and I know the option of a flight is there if I need to go home. But my husband and daughter are in the UK. My home is here. I'm happy, but there is a tugging feeling, and I expect that will always be there.

There isn't a solution. It's just the situation.

What other expats have to say

Amanda, an American living in the UK
There's guilt and sadness when you're so far from home and disconnected from the day-to-day issues. It heightens the feeling of regret and guilt when you miss important moments and time with your family.

Anon, a Brit living in Argentina
I was a chronic nail biter all my life before I came here. I feel so happy and settled here that I stopped biting my nails.

Anon, a Brit who has lived in Ivory Coast, Benin, Israel, France, China and Senegal
My mum died when we were on our first posting in Ivory Coast. I felt powerless and so sad that I hadn't seen her since the summer. She died on 7 November and they were supposed to be coming to stay on 10 November.

Rebecca, who is Irish, living in Singapore, married to an Australian
This is an example of how multicultural our kids are, with so many friends whose parents are from different countries:
Son: "Where is Chris from?"
Me: "Australia."
Son: "And where is his wife from?"
Me: "Australia."
Son: "The same place?!"

Me: "Yes, Sydney."
Son: "Why would they marry each other if they come from the same place? How boring!"

Where do you start?

- It sometimes helps you to feel more settled if you have a "get out plan" – even if you're just tricking your mind. As soon as you can, book your flight home for a holiday. It helps reassure family at home that they will see you again, and gives you something to look forward to.

- Have coffee with other expat friends. It really helps to be able to have a moan and get it off your chest. They will probably be feeling the same way so they won't be judging you.

- Part of the expat journey is about acceptance. You will feel guilty, and if you want to live away from your homeland that is just the reality of the situation. However, if you stayed near family and never travelled you'd probably feel stifled and have itchy feet.

National identity

You've made a positive leap into the unknown, to live abroad for the first time: very excited, maybe a little daunted and certainly somewhat bewildered. All the while you're intoxicated by the exotic new sights, sounds and smells of your new abode, your mind is subconsciously rearranging your thoughts and opinions about your homeland. You first start to struggle to work out your new self-identity, which is influenced by your unfamiliar surroundings. Then your mind starts to work out what your national identity means to you, when literally viewed from a different location. Do you still see you home nation in the same way?

For some, this means hanging their coat of arms on the front door, or running the flag up the pole every morning, wearing a pith helmet and knobbly knees. For others, it means keeping their nation's traditions alive for their children, or perhaps even under a misunderstanding that everyone else must celebrate them too. (I was once asked by an American what we called Independence Day, on 4th July, in the UK. They weren't too impressed when I answered "Tuesday", and even less impressed that we should let such an auspicious date go by without some flag waving, until I pointed out it I would be akin to ... hang on, there is no akin. Who celebrates a war they've lost?!)

The more you try to analyse why you're keeping these traditions alive, the more confused the mind gets. It's really important for children to understand their heritage. It's also really important to ensure your patriotism doesn't become jingoism. We all become defensive, which only fuels a need to celebrate our own country's strong points louder and louder and louder, until we've insulted all our neighbours and start to feel a little embarrassed about our homeland.

Expats generally see themselves as citizens of the world[23], and leaving patriotism aside, understand that they are in no place to judge when they are working and living in someone else's country.

So that's where the waters get muddied. Expats are also a sector of society that protect their own traditions and, acting as ambassadors, protect their country's reputation abroad.

An identity is a community of similar, like-minded people. We can't be cookie cutter nations, otherwise what is the point of nation states in the first place? My children have lived in four countries and they know that the world is made up of all colours, all religions, all cultures. And that's all ok. As my older daughter said: "We all have two arms, two legs and one head, but we aren't the same."

Children often have a unique way of looking at the world because they don't have any preconceived ideas. More than 95%[24] of expats thinks that children benefit from life abroad, citing greater cultural, political, linguistic understanding and lifelong friends from diverse backgrounds as reasons. It is also thought that exposure to new cultures expands a child's understanding of the world, and broadens their empathy towards those who at first seem different. This increases their level of tolerance.

For more than 50%[25] of expats a child's lack of national identity is a worry. They noted that it was harder to answer the question "where are you from and where is your home?". One mother said that children: "miss out on some quintessential experiences about

---

[23] Expat Explorers' survey: The greatest number of expats are in Singapore, the UK, the UAE and the US.
[24] Expat Explorers' survey: 96% of 675 respondents.
[25] Expat Explorers' survey: 52% of 675 respondents.

growing up in their home culture that could connect them with their compatriots. But they gain so much more, so it's a net win."

Interestingly, less than 7%[26] of expats said culture was the main thing they missed about home, with one person stating: "For me, it was the familiarity of everything that was missing, rather than one specific thing."

Nearly a third of expats[27] thought a new cultural experience was the top advantage of being an expat. Only 1% said it was the main disadvantage.

National identity is about celebrating our differences, while not denting our growth in our new community. Here's an example: I don't know why we still measure road distances in miles in the UK, when we have been part of a metric system the entire four decades I've been on this planet. It makes no sense, and only complicates issues when I drive in other countries. However, when I go to the pub, I may like to have a pint. It's a quintessentially British measure, and changes nothing else. The world does not shift on its axis. Nothing else is measured in a pint. I don't have to convert it. It's just a pint.

Stereotypes develop when enough people propagate a behaviour. During the 1950s and 1960s, the bowler hat was part of the British businessman's uniform. We don't wear them anymore, but I bet if someone says "British businessman" you mind conjures up an image of a straight-backed gentleman in a pin-striped suit with a bowler hat, black umbrella and briefcase (or it will now I've suggested it!). We don't sit down to an afternoon tea of scones and cream every day, more's the pity, but 165 million cups of tea are still

---

[26] Expat Explorers' survey: 7% of 675 respondents.
[27] Expat Explorers' survey: 33% of 675 respondents.

drunk in the UK every day.[28]

Not all stereotypes are correct. I've never actually heard an Australian say: "put another shrimp on the barbie", especially as my Aussie friends call them prawns. And I've never seen a Frenchman on a bicycle with a string of onions around his neck.

Our personal identity is intrinsically linked to our national identity. It helps us to make sense of the world. But, we're a transient part of society. We're expats. We often live unsettled or unstable lives, not knowing when we're going to be moved again. There is comfort in having an identity and a culture you can cling to, something that is constant.

So, what does this all mean? To me, it means that developing your own personality and individualism is something your parents taught you when you were growing up. As long as it doesn't impact other people it's fine. The same goes for our national identity and the development of our cultural communities - as long as they are inclusive and aren't racist. It shouldn't say: "Stay out, we don't want you to join our gang." It should be an excuse to say: "Hey, we're a bit difference. Come and join us for a cup of tea and some scones."

---

[28] According to the UK Tea and Infusions Association, whose, er, job it is to promote tea. https://www.tea.co.uk/tea-faqs

Meet Jacqueline

Jacqueline is from New Zealand and has lived abroad for eight years, in Singapore and the US. Having children while living in the US has meant making conscious decisions about the cultural elements that influence their upbringing.

When we first moved to Singapore, we felt like Kiwis and hung out with Kiwis. We watched the Rugby World Cup together, we attended BBQs at one another's homes, and one of the invitees usually made some typically Kiwi food, such as onion dip, pavlova or lolly cake. Honestly, I didn't even eat those things when I lived in New Zealand - but they are definitely delicious, and were a great source of bonding.

I felt like more of a Kiwi in the first few years of being away. In New York, we don't feel "Kiwi". We are not treated any differently, just sometimes people can't understand our accent so we have to slow down. We also have to use the American versions of words in order to be understood, for example, sidewalk instead of footpath, squash or zucchini instead of courgette.

Singapore isn't too far from New Zealand, and is under the Asia Pacific umbrella, so most people had a good understanding of the country and its news. It was a conversation starter, and Singaporeans, or people from other countries, often relied heavily on what they knew about New Zealand, telling us how much they love it or wanted to go there.

My national identity changed the longer I lived abroad. That may be because we moved to New York, where almost no one is local. It's a true melting pot of cultures, and most people are transplants from other countries or states. Almost nobody talks about "home" and compares it to New York. Perhaps that's because there is a feeling that New York is home, for now anyway. No one seems to know how long they will be here, whereas in Singapore most people were on two-year contracts, or they were planning to leave at some point.

Our accent doesn't necessarily stick out in New York because there are so many accents. Someone may occasionally ask about it, or think we're Australian, but people don't have much time for small talk, so the conversation soon grinds to a halt. Cultural reference points are different too. In Singapore, we'd be asked about rugby and cricket. Neither of those sports are recognised here, so people might reference an element of popular culture, such as Flight of the Concords or a celebrity.

If people use stereotypes to connect with us, it usually means they are Brits, Aussies, South Africans or from another Commonwealth country. Singaporeans and Americans don't tend to joke about us, probably because they don't feel they know enough to do so.

We know a handful of Kiwis here, but we haven't sought out a Kiwi contingent like we did in Singapore. I'm not sure if that's because we have been away longer or if it's because our friends share the 'expat' mentality - 90% of them were raised outside New York City and moved here as adults, so their families are far away too.

What we think about home has changed too. While living in Singapore, we thought New Zealand was cold, whereas now we're in New York we think New Zealand has an eternal summer compared to the brutal winters here. We are committed to going outdoors, rain, snow or shine. Our love of the outdoors is the main aspect of New Zealand culture we are hoping to pass on to our American accented children. That said, many of our American friends here are also looking for that lifestyle for their children.

We haven't tried to replicate our Kiwi life here though. We have tried to embrace the local traditions of the country we are in, for example, Chinese New Year and Diwali in Singapore, and Thanksgiving, Valentine's Day and Hallowe'en in the US. Sometimes I do need to call a friend to get some cultural advice.

For example, the kids here make Valentines for one another for Valentine's

Day, and I needed to know whether that was a card or a gift, as where I'm from the day is usually a celebration for couples. Hallowe'en is also more of an event here. It took us a few years to realise that it wasn't about scary costumes and tricks. Most people in the US dress in fun costumes, as a homage to their favourite people or characters.

We have always had the mentality of "we are not going to be here forever so let's make the most of it." We intend to take these celebrations back to New Zealand when we eventually return.

Being from New Zealand has both helped and hindered us. I work in marketing and public relations so my written language skills were in demand in Singapore, especially among companies with an international reach. However, many organisations also wanted to support local talent so it could be a hindrance in terms of picking up contracts. A lot of expats work with expats for that reason. In the US, I've mainly had a neutral experience, but I'm pretty certain I missed out on a role in a company that wanted an American accent, possibly because it was a client-facing position.

We try to create the right balance between our national identities and are lucky to have been able to go home to New Zealand once a year. We say "home" when we go, even though we have lived abroad for eight years. It always feels funny for about a day, but it still feels like home. When we are in New Zealand, we are 100% back to being Kiwi, and the kids live like Kiwis. When we are back in New York, we slip back into American routines, but I think it's important not to compare which is better, this home or that home, because they are both good, just different.

What other expats have to say

Ali, a Brit who has lived in Canada, Egypt, Hong Kong, India, China and Myanmar

We've always given our children some help and preparation with answering the question: "Where are you from?" It's tricky for them and can be tricky for others too. I find that question increasingly hard to answer. I am a sum of all my experiences and carry a little bit of all my countries with me. I have a vivid memory of my daughter at about three, with sun-bleached hair, wearing a shalwar chemise and insisting (to the amusement of some enquiring Indians) that she was an Indian girl, and she lived in India.

Anon, Australian, who has lived in Indonesia, Iran and Doha

Put yourself out there and experience the flavours of the country. Don't lose your identity but stay true to who you are. Be open to advice or new ideas. Remember to save some money for when you come back home. Purchase a home in your home country and rent it out while you are away. It's amazing how your home country grows while you are not there.

Dave, a Brit, who has lived in UAE, Canada, Hong Kong, Brunei and Nigeria

Growing up with other children of different nationalities and cultures gives them a broader outlook.

Abby, a Brit who has lived in Germany, Switzerland, China and USA

I had so many cultural mishaps – but seeing my two sons now being able to connect with people from all over the world is pretty special. They look for that point of connection.

Where do you start?

- Write a list of all the national holidays and traditions from your home nation and those from your host nation. Now choose the best bits and create your own national identity.

- Choose a public holiday or custom you don't understand and research its history.

- Write down all the funny things children say when they are confused about their nationality. It's a great way to make memories. When we returned to the UK my daughter got into a panic on her first day of school. She came home and asked me to "teach her the words to the national anthem as it's a different tune and I only know it in Mandarin".

Local connections

Being "settled" means different things to different people. For some, it is about finding out where to buy the foods they like from home, or choosing a house and school. For others, it can be a deeper understanding of how their new home ticks, finding ways to connect with the local environment. Nearly a third of people surveyed named cultural experience as the top advantage to expat life[29].

Let's take "the wild man" as an example. This is a tale of coincidence, intrigue and fate; how many times can a man you've never met cross your path?

To the Japanese, he was known as "the tall man who never slept". To me, he was one of the heroes of the Second World War.

Major, later Colonel, Cyril Wild carried the British white surrender flag to the front line when Singapore fell to the Japanese on that fateful day in February 1942. However, not one cell belonging to this man surrendered that day.

My fascination with Wild started when we moved to Singapore in 2013. Being interested in military history, I wanted to find out if the land we were living on had played a part in any battles, as it was opposite Dempsey Hill barracks. I also wanted to find some connection with my local surroundings. What I discovered was that we were just a kilometre from the front line.

---

[29] Expat Explorers' survey: The top three advantages to expat life are cultural experience (32%), being financially better off (26%) and travel (16%).

In photographs taken at the time, I first met Major Wild, alongside Lieutenant General Arthur Percival, the General Officer Commanding, marching to the surrender spot. He was carrying the white flag. There is nothing to mark the soil that played such a pivotal part in the start of the end of the British Empire, except a dual carriageway and a flyover.

The following year I celebrated my 40th birthday and my long-suffering husband asked me what I wanted to do for the day. I decided that a visit to the Ford Factory, the location of the surrender signing and now a museum, would be the ideal way to mark the day. My husband rolled his eyes. In truth, on any other day I wasn't likely to find many people to share my interest. It was at the museum that I came face to face with Major Cyril Wild, or to be exact a mannequin. This time he was holding the Union flag.

Wild served the rest of the conflict as a prisoner of war (POW), both at Changi prison and later on the Thai-Burmese railway, known blackly as the Death Railway. Nearly 13,000 Allied POWs lost their life building it.

The conditions were harsh. Food was limited, sanitation non-existent and the physical labour was backbreaking. Wild's first priority was to his men. As an officer, the Japanese respected his rank and nicknamed him "the tall man who never slept", a nod to his dedication to his soldiers. He was also useful as he spoke Japanese, having worked in Japan with the Shell oil company.

His loyalty to his men, and his ability to communicate with his captors, saved the lives of many. One man forever in his debt was James Bradbury, a British Royal Engineer who tried to escape from the Thai-Burmese railway, despite knowing that the penalty upon capture was death. In charge of cremations at an isolation camp, and as a cholera carrier himself, he had little to lose.

Some escapees perished, but Bradbury and five others managed to last six weeks in the jungle before they were discovered by two Burmese hunters - and sold back to the Japanese. Wild saved Bradbury from execution by arguing his case.

Wild survived the war. During his captivity, he took a great risk in concealing the Union Flag, which he had held during the surrender signing. He was asked to hand it over, but told the Japanese that it has been burnt.

In September 1945, after Japan's surrender, Lord Mountbatten, the Supreme Allied Commander South East Asia, invited Wild to hoist the flag over Singapore's town hall.

The following year, he was due to return to Singapore as a war crimes liaison officer. Tragically, his plane crashed, and all 19 crew and passengers died. The official report concluded that the crash had been caused by turbulence. However, a subsequent conspiracy theory is that the plane was sabotaged as Wild was a key witness in the war crimes trials. The Western worry was that the complete collapse of the imperial Japanese family would create a power vacuum, attracting communism.

The Union flag was tracked down by Wild's brothers. As a memorial, it was laid to rest in the Charterhouse School Chapel, in Godalming, Wild's old school and my hometown. It has now found a permanent, respectful resting place in the Imperial War Museum, London.

However, Wild was to cross my path one more time. At a family gathering I was talking to Christian, a friend of my mother's. They had trained together as nurses in the 1960s. I knew her surname was Wild. I didn't know that she was Cyril Wild's niece.

This story has come full circle. I've visited the Imperial War

Museum with Christian, and seen the flag on display. To me it's an iconic, tangible piece of history that symbolises the demise of the British Empire. The threads of the flag and its history run deep. This flag, and its story, helped me to understand a little more about Singapore's past, and its social and political development.

Travel has made me inquisitive. It's a journey of investigation, where the aim is to find out how we fit into the world's jigsaw. Expat life has taught me that this world is small. Countless times I have met people who know people that I know. Even through history, there is a connection to others. And, to me, that's a wonderful thought.

Meet Jon

Digging around in the Singaporean soil gave Jon Cooper, a battlefield archaeologist, the opportunity to not only learn more about his adoptive country and make local connections, but to explore how national identity and our environment are intrinsically linked.

Singapore, which celebrated its 50th birthday in 2015, is a melting pot of cultures, with four official languages – Tamil, Malay, Mandarin and English. In a modern age of unpredictable cataclysms, patriotism is the glue that holds the nation together, but that's a difficult concept in a country with many identities.

Understanding the history of where we live is one way to start to develop an understanding of who you are and where you came from, but that's not always an easy journey. Singapore is a bit like a teenager embarrassed by its colonial parents, especially when they were found to be not as perfect as they had made out to be. There is little succour to be had in the fact that the British sacrificed so much to reinstate its duties. It was simply expected of them as responsible parents.

As time passes you forget the embarrassment and remember the love and sacrifice of your parents. Later you aspire to be like them, albeit with a modern twist and marvellous skyscrapers. At very least you learn from their experiences. But to do so you must have some memory of who they were and what life was like back then.

As a visiting battlefield archaeologist, my job was to dig around the darkest recesses of the attic for things those parents may have left behind. It all felt a tad uncomfortable. I was, however, oblivious to all that when I first set out to survey the battlefields of Singapore. I trundled merrily along digging up ammunition, identifying lost gravesites and revealing hidden chapel murals. I naturally assumed that people would be interested, no matter their nationality, and recalling such history would be welcomed.

The Singaporean authorities, however, thought I was just crazy, annoying or a combination of both.

Soon, I knew more about the local area than the taxi drivers, and began to receive invites to garden parties to talk to guests about the vicious hand to hand fighting that had taken place by the swimming pool. Telling a good story in any language is worth its weight in gold and great way to break down the barriers.

Now I was able to contribute something to my adopted homeland, and give something back. My Singaporean friends now introduced me as: "Ang Moh[30]... but he is OK."

The greatest thrill was to bring Singaporean school kids onto dig sites and watch as they dug out their first bullet. Their careful shovelling, the instant of recognition of what they had found, and the incredulity that spread across their faces from ear to ear, as they proudly showed the bullet to their mates, was something to behold.

"We never knew," was a common comment, "Nobody told us this happened here."

The Singapore education system had failed to share this vibrant and compelling story. But what was more disconcerting was that this was 'shared' heritage, something the Brits and Australians would travel thousands of miles to indulge in, but was lost to the very people who had been entrusted in its upkeep and protection.

"Well, it's not 'our' history," the older generations would say. "It didn't really have anything to do with us. It was a foreign war on our land – we just kept our heads down."

Perhaps, but heritage is not uniquely associated with people. Heritage is

---

[30] Ang Moh is Hokkien for "red-haired" or white man, sometimes used in a mildly derogatory way.

also embedded in landscape and location. It would be like most of Europe asking: "What have the Romans ever done for us?" You are who you are not only because of race but also because of your environment.

In contrast, selling the value of heritage to a young nation is like selling pensions to teenagers – they simply can't see the point. With endless possibilities stretching out before them, Singapore has no time to worry about where it came from, only where it's going.

Equally, a passion for local or colonial history may not necessarily always be a good thing. It's easy to follow well-trodden paths of nationalistic propaganda and engrained jingoism mapped out by the prevailing authority. Propaganda is rife and selected history is used to justify current events. It's a powerful and dangerous resource in the wrong hands.

A lot of military history is about misunderstanding and mistrust. It is political and emotive, and a study of the best and worst of mankind. Nonetheless, military heritage can be used to heal, to understand, to share common experiences, to help forgiveness and to learn from the past.

What other expats have to say

Natalie, from France, has lived in the UAE, Singapore, Indonesia, Iran and Saudi Arabia

Expat communities are made of people who are all in the same situation, for example, moving around and rebuilding their lives constantly, seeking new friendships- it is therefore easy to meet people. Maybe not so easy with local people. In some countries they do not mingle easily, for example Gulf countries, and in some others there might be language barriers... but we usually manage to meet some great locals.

Anon, Hungarian living in the UK
Keep calm and be ready to adopt the local culture.

Meet Elise

Elise is an American living in Britain

After living in the UK for about 18 months, my former flatmate messaged to me saying that I kept getting letters, and she didn't know why.

It turns out I hadn't paid a parking fine and it was being sent to my old address. I had updated my driver's licence address, but didn't realise that in the UK you also have to write to the DVLA [driving authority] stating you've moved.

The parking ticket for £3.50 was not paid for over a year, and had grown to over £1,000!

It was my fault for not knowing that I had to change my address separately. I remember sitting on the floor opening over 20 letters from the parking authority, from debt collectors, with warnings, missed summons to court. It was such a mess!

After getting over the shock, I called all of the people and explained the situation. Over and over I appealed all the tickets, went to several court appearances, and even cried on the phone to the debt collectors.

In the end, I ended up paying just the original fine at £3.50. It just goes to show, people are willing to be gracious if you take the time to understand.

My advice is be honest with other people. I never thought British people, with all their rules and regulations, would understand my mistake, but they did. It was a hugely empowering turning point realising that I can in fact navigate the culture.

Anon, Taiwanese living in the UAE
Be aware of the local culture and the legal obligations and limitations; embrace the culture and don't stay within the bubble of familiarities.

Anon, an America living in Singapore
It's been very difficult to make friends with local people because their lifestyle is much different to my own and our times/interests/values don't align well enough for them to take time to get to know me. Or for me to create a lasting bond.

Anthea, an Australian who has lived in Malaysia
If I had my expat time again, I would learn the language and learn more about the history and culture of the place. All of our three kids were born while we were expats in Malaysia, so it was a busy time and it didn't leave much time for me to do the things I wanted to do.

Fiona, a Brit living in the US
Don't hide away in an expat enclave. Make friends with the locals.

Where do you start?

- Search for local history interest groups – it's a good way to meet new people. Museums and Facebook are a good place to start.

- Research the history of your new home, starting with military, economic, social, architectural, or even the etymology of the language.

- Go the library, or if you're lucky, national archives, and dig out some photos of how your new home used to look 50 or 100 years ago. Pick up your camera and try to replicate the shots so you can see how things have changed.

Packing up

"What have you been doing all day?" my darling husband says as he walks through the door, after a long day at work. He doesn't mean it as an accusation, but I take it as one.

Yesterday, our freight arrived. I have two little children running round and round tall looming towers of boxes, stacked so high they are starting to sway in the wind. There are 381 of them. It's all very well that the removal company offer a "surface unpacking service" (i.e. they will put things on surfaces, but not in cupboards), but there are no surfaces. Every inch is covered with piles of random stuff. Despite my finely honed organisational skills, there's a toothbrush and a pile of toiletries by the kitchen sink, a bike in my lounge and a dolls' house in my bedroom.

I'm famous for my lists, but my system has failed me. The process is no longer under my control. Take this example: We were allowed a limited amount of air freight, so I packed the essentials I thought we'd need, including bedding for the first night. I clearly labelled what it was. I even showed the removal company's foreman, so he was aware.

We arrived at our destination and opened the air freight. There was no bedding. On the bright side, I did have what looked like a box of flotsam and jetsam, scrapped off my daughter's bedroom floor: a pencil, a small bear, a broken piece of plastic, a dice, a single glove from the dressing up box, a book and a ball of fluff. This was obviously junk that had been swept from under the bed. A joke or incompetence? You decide.

The sea freight arrived eight weeks later. The vital "first night" bedding was found, divided between boxes four, 23 and 321. I can't even begin to think how this actually happened and can only put it down to bored packers with Machiavellian tendencies.

Six months after our kit arrived in Dubai, sitting in the garden, we found a roughly-wrapped package sellotaped under our garden table. We unwrapped it gingerly, and that's how I found my mascara and lipstick, long-since thought lost forever. Again, I cannot understand how….

Unpacking and packing up are difficult experiences. It's not just the physical, monotonous nature of putting items into boxes. It's the brain power that it involves, even if you have a removal company to help you.

Usually, a move follows a familiar pattern:
1. Panic;
2. Acceptance of the imminent move;
3. Writing a list of all the things you want to do and see before you leave;
4. Writing a list of all the things you want to sell/ get rid of;
5. Writing a list of all the things you'll need at your destination to help you manage before your freight arrives;
6. Writing a list of all the things you need to do, people you need to inform in both the country you're leaving and heading to;
7. Writing a list of all the things you need to pack in a suitcase to take with you;
8. Moving items around the house so they are in the right rooms;
9. Rewriting all lists;
10. Feeling overwhelmed;
11. Resorting to a large glass of gin, or if the glasses have been packed, a bottle with a straw.

It gets so complicated I even had to keep a spreadsheet and Gantt chart, so I knew what was happening and when. It's difficult to understate the administration required. You go to bed with your mind swirling and wake up in the middle of the night in a sweat because you've just remembered you need to sort out school places/ forgotten to send out the leaving party invites/ need to find transport for Dave the dog.

Of course, removal and relocation companies help a great deal, but there has to be a project manager. If the move is with your partner's job, or you're moving on your own, that will be you.

In rare circumstances, you may have to pack up very suddenly. When we lived in Dubai, we were concerned about the US elections, and the impact of living in a country with a US military base and a fairly hostile neighbour. Call us over prepared, but we had a "go bag", which contained some cash, passports, toothbrushes, underwear and emergency teddy bear. We had an escape route and we knew what we were going to do should the waste product hit the proverbial fan.

All this packing stress, trepidation and pain is laced with anticipation and excitement too. What will the next adventure be like? They say: "no pain, no gain", but there are so many of us moving around all the time, does it have to be so stressful? Surely someone must have got this situation licked?

Meet Karen

Karen, a Brit who has lived in the US and Thailand, has packed her home into boxes 14 times in 17 years. With the skill down to a fine art, she was able to swiftly evacuate her family from Bangkok during political violence in May 2010, putting the problems of packing into perspective.

We had been living in Thailand for several months when anti-government protests, involving the Red-shirts and Yellow-shirts, reached boiling point. It was a scary situation that really put life into perspective. We were watching daily for communications about the political situation from our embassy and were advised to carry cash and passports at all times. This situation continued for weeks so became our new "normal".

However, overnight things changed. There were no police on the streets, and no security. Protesters were throwing blood at the Prime Minister's house, only a few doors down from my youngest child's nursery, which went into lock down. It was a very stressful time.

Very suddenly, and almost without warning, there was fighting just two streets from our house. My husband phoned and told me he was evacuating the office, and we should be ready to go, but he didn't know for how long. I was given twenty minutes to pack up. The main worry was that traffic was gridlocked and there were tanks in the road. It took several hours to reach the nursery to pick my daughter up. My two oldest children were travelling home on the school bus as tanks were driving on the same freeway and protesters started firing at them. The military just took over.

When the situation is on a knife-edge like that packing is very easy. Basically, it's passports, cash and photographs. Everything else can be replaced, although today I wouldn't even need to pack photographs.

Eventually we were on the road out of the city, with the children in the car. At one point, surrounded by black tyre smoke, we were stopped by a road block. A soldier with a rifle searched our car, even checking under the children's teddy bears in their car seats.

On top of that our driver smelled strongly of drink, but that seemed to be the least of our worries as we left the burning city and uncertainty behind us. He had been drinking, as the situation was so stressful, and he didn't expect to have to go anywhere, but we relied on him as the only way we could get around.

My husband's job meant that he was in charge of the region for his company, and so he was responsible for his staff. That meant he was the last to leave.

We stayed with friends 40 miles north of the city, for three weeks, until it was safe enough to come home. At the time you just grab and go. There isn't any time to make decisions. You're a fish out of water and vulnerable.

People think you're very lucky to be an expat, but rarely see the other side of it.

What other expats have to say

Anon, a Jamaican who has lived in the UK, Belgium and the US
My mother was an expat for many years and has tales of the Commonwealth Wives' Club providing linen, dinner and tea services complete with silver tea pots to tide you over until your freight arrived. My, times have changed since the 1950s and 1960s. I'm not sure that even exists anymore. Thank God for Ikea.

Meet Emma

Emma is a Brit living in the Netherlands

After we had been here a year we had to move out of our house and find alternative accommodation. Rentable houses are few and far between, particularly around the Christmas period. We felt very pressured to find a place, so we ended up going for somewhere that we knew on first inspection was fairly rough and ready, but we were prepared to get in and do a bit of painting.

As we began to move our stuff in, we realised what a massive mistake we'd made! The house had mice, it had been left in quite a filthy state and there were significant issues with the plumbing. We were left trying to find alternative accommodation.

Thankfully we had made some very good friends who stepped in and saved the day. Two couples had us stay with them in the run up to the holidays and another couple let us stay at their place while they went home to Ireland.

Quite aside from the practicalities they all provided much needed shoulders to cry on. I think expat living makes you realise that you are all in it together, away from your own families and friends, so you find like-minded others that give you the emotional support you need in tricky situations. I will forever be very grateful for having known them.

Malcolm, a Brit now living in Ireland, who has lived in 10 countries
My wife and I have now moved and made homes in 44 different locations – sometimes several in same city.

Susie, a Brit living in the US
We still have boxes, that have moved to a new country four times, that have never been opened in between! I have no idea what is in them.

Where do you start?

Here are Karen's top packing tips:
Sort and chuck! When moving, possessions become "stuff" and too much stuff can cause extra stress, so be ruthless. Your moving package may have shipment size limitations too. Does that bright pink plastic dollshouse, that hasn't been played with in months, really need a plane ticket? Having a good sort out means you are in a good place emotionally. While in the process of saying goodbye to family and friends you are more likely to hang on to the never used fondue set that Aunty Gladys got you for Christmas "just because". House plants will not survive an international move, and are not usually allowed, so give them away.

Make a movie. Video your entire house contents so nothing is missed. Paperwork for a move can be immense, starting with the itemised inventory, which sometimes doesn't even bear a resemblance to your belongings, making insurance claims very difficult. My friend's shipment was sat in the dock in Louisiana as Hurricane Katrina hit and they lost everything. Take photographs of display cabinets, bookshelves and the rat's nest of wires out the back of the computer, so you can see how things can be pieced back together at the other end. Scan all important certificates and documents and save them to a portable hard drive or cloud.

Create a no-pack zone. The packing team will pack everything unless told otherwise, including the entire contents of the junk drawer, mushed boiled sweets and all. Nobody wants to hunt for your handbag in 300 packed boxes. Keep your suitcases, air shipment, important documents, kettle/teabags/mugs etc. in the no-pack zone. Colour coded stickers are useful, for example, red = don't pack, yellow = to storage, blue = charity shop. I also have a remote-control box clearly marked and ensure all remotes are placed in there, and also include a few spare batteries. Make sure the tool box is labelled as it will be needed quickly when unpacking.

Make your bed and lie in it. Ask the packers for a box so you can pack a clean set of bedding for each bed (and towels) so that on the day of unpacking at least you can get the beds made up for a good night's rest. Put a big red ribbon around this/ decorate it with Christmas wrapping paper or anything else that will make this box stand out.

Where are the screws?! I ask the packers to tape a sealable plastic bag to each shelving unit/bed for all screws and fixings for ease of assembly at the other end. Make sure they don't stick it on surface or areas that could be damaged though.

Forbidden fruit. Discuss with the packing team leader if they are allowed to pack dry food goods, herbs and spices, alcohol or perfume, as at one time or another my packers have refused to pack one or all of these items and this can be expensive.

How will it work? Find out whether transformers or adaptor plugs are needed in your new home country. Do you need to take the television if it's the wrong frequency? Is it safer to purchase new goods? Check the availability of items that Amazon deliver. I arrived in Thailand unaware that tampons or "feminine hygiene products" were not readily available so stock up on what you need.

Label it. Put a large label on the door of each room with corresponding labels on the boxes, for example Tom's bedroom, kitchen etc.

So, you've arrived! You may have been living out of a suitcase in a hotel for a few weeks, while house hunting. Or twiddling your thumbs in your new home just counting down the days until the sea shipment arrives with your "stuff". You may have had a village of friends and family to help with the packing and childcare in your home country. Welcome to expat life - you are on your own!

Obviously, the working spouse will have some "very important, cannot possible get out of meeting" to attend. So, the task will rest with you and your packing team, who may, or may not, speak your language.

Label it again. Label the rooms of your new accommodation with the same labelling system you used when you packed. Do a mental assessment to ensure everything will fit in as planned. Give the kitchen storage a look over in a calmer time as you'll only want to unpack those plates once.

Housey, housey! You will be needed to check off the boxes as they arrive. Just think of this as a mega game of bingo with numbers being randomly shouted at you.

Unpack it. You have a couple of options. Say goodbye to the moving company or pay for an unpacking service. The latter is not always as helpful as you may think though. Most companies will not put goods away. They simply unwrap them and place them on floor or a surface. This service has limited value as I have quickly found they run out of surfaces and floorspace, leaving you unable to move, with precariously placed ornaments wobbling above children crawling on the floor. However, the reconstruction of furniture is very helpful, and with all nuts and bolts accounted for, it should be seamless!!

Good luck.

Repating

Repating – permanently returning home to your home country – can be as much of a challenge as expating. Nearly 50% of people find it difficult[31]. Knowledge and experience of your homeland means you have fixed preconceived ideas and memories, even if they are buried deep in your subconscious. That's not always helpful. It hard to see whether it's the jigsaw that has changed or whether it's your piece in it.

The definition of the word "repat" is changing. A contracted form of the word "repatriate", it traditionally means sending a person back to their country of citizenship. I would go even further and say that it has become an experience in its own right.

There are plenty of books telling you how to live abroad, but a few new titles are creeping onto the shelves, exploring the experience, issues, trials and tribulations of returning home.

When you leave home for a stint overseas your return journey is the furthest thought from your mind, and it stays there. For many people, the thought comes to the fore too late and they are already knee-deep in trouble, with an inner voice shouting: "It was supposed to be great. It was supposed to be easy."

Repating can be just as difficult as settling into an unknown land. Of course, you don't have the language barrier. Or do you? Of course, you still have friends. Or do you? Of course, you've returned a more interesting person with a wealth of stories and experiences to share. Or have you?

---

[31] Expat Explorers' survey: 48% of people found repating a challenge.

Language

Let's start with communication. I was brought up speaking English. Moving home was supposed to be a piece of cake, but I suddenly found myself surrounded by new words, terms and brand names I didn't recognise. Take my first trip to the supermarket. It all looked the same. I queued patiently at the check out, as only a Brit can do, confident that I had not lost these inherent skills. At last, it was my turn and I started to stack my shopping on the conveyor belt.

Suddenly, a hand slapped down and I was admonished in a rather loud voice by the check-out assistant: "You can't do that here," she bellowed. Other shoppers turned to see what all the kerfuffle was about, meercats peeking above the heads of others, probably expecting to see me naked, performing a pole dance in the ailse. (I wasn't.) I racked my brain to try to identify my misdemeanor. In a quizical fashion, I looked at the lady who had scolded me. "This is Fast Track," she added. That's ok. I'm happy to go fast.

Seeing I hadn't moved a muscle, she began to speak more slowly, and loudly. "F-a-s-t T-r-a-ck." It didn't help that I replied: "What's that?" If she wasn't sure whether I was stupid before, it appears she had apparently just had her suspicions confirmed. Fast Track, it turns out, is a service you register for, giving you the right to be your own check-out assistant by scanning your items as you go. At the end of your shop you hand over the scanner and forego the tedious task of taking everything out of your trolley only to put them back in again.

The problem is I had been away so long, processes and words had changed. Having a British accent people assumed I knew what was going on. For the first six months I felt in a state of flux, faking my local knowledge in some situations, while using it to my advantage in others. (I'm still wondering how long I can get away with this.)

Thank goodness for friends who put up with endless messages asking: "What doesn't such and such mean?" It's a confusing world we live in to the uninitiated, and repats.

Friends and family

Relationships are often another area where repats stumble. You catch up with the same people who were your friends before you left, having kept in touch through social media and the odd Christmas card. You start to feel that it's nice to slot back in.

Except you haven't. The jigsaw hole you left has been filled, or the puzzle may be an entirely different picture. Your friends have stood still and moved on all at the same time. You've packed your life full of very different experiences, so maybe the shape of your own jigsaw piece has changed and you don't fit in anymore.

You can make the same assumptions with family. I love my siblings dearly, but I had to remind myself that we'd only really been in touch a couple of times a year. We're all pretty rubbish about picking up the phone, just for a chat, and in some of the places I've lived, this technology wasn't even reliably available. It can be an entirely, and unexpectantly, complicated process just to say hello. The first step is to send an email to set up a time to call, remembering the time difference. After school runs, work, the children's party you forgot about and dinner time, this will probably mean that the only opportunity to speak will be 23 minutes on a Tuesday during the second week of February.

You try to video call but, inevitably, it will be shaky so you'll compromise by having a voice call; only to find out you've got a powercut or the broadband has failed altogether.

It's not just the technological disadvantage that expat life dumps at your door. It's the issues of the relationship themselves. You have to remind yourself that you were the one who went away. You have to give yourself time to recollect the pattern and personality of different conversations and relationships. You have to work hard at something most people don't even think about.

A new culture

One aspect I hadn't expected was introducing my children to a new culture. They were born in Britain. They had visited Britain on a number of occasions. It hadn't occurred to me that culturally they were not British. Here's a couple of examples:

Example 1
Daughter: "What's the Bible?"

Example 2
Teacher: "This is how you spell the months of year. Please put them in the four boxes for the four seasons."
Look of horror on daughter's face.
Teacher: "What's the matter? It's an easy task."
Daughter: "I don't know what seasons are."

These examples possibly mean that you are now judging my parenting skills, but in my defence, my daughters were immersing themselves in the local culture, and religion, and had never seen autumn or spring. They didn't lack knowledge. They just had different knowledge.

Finally, let's look at the insights and experience your expat life has given you. It's fine to feel proud about all that you have seen, and learnt, but there's a tipping point. Don't come to be known as the "when we weres". It's really hard to avoid the temptation to start a sentence with: "When were were in Thailand/ Australia/ Outer

Mongolia..." Conversations often draw on personal experience and views, but it's not always something that others can't relate to.

In what may be an apocryphal story, a friend of my husband came back to Dubai from a trip home having decided that it was time to repat. The reason? In a pub conversation, his friends had asked him what the worst part of his life was. He answered truthfully, unfortunately: the worst part of his life was that his swimming pool was too warm to use year-round, and he was considering installing a chiller to make it usable in the 50 degree heat of a Dubai summer. His friends responded in the best British way possible – and spent the rest of the night mocking him mercilessly. Within three months he and his family returned home, where they are enviably happy, despite not having a pool.

There we have it. You will feel like a stranger in your own country. The way of life will have changed. The roads will be busier. Prices will have gone up. However, as each month goes by, you will assimilate, and you'll do this more quickly if you accept that you may have to remould your jigsaw piece.

Meet Niki

To some repating is the experience of coming full circle, back to the bosom of family and friends. To others it can be a traumatic experience, which leaves you longing for your expat life.

Niki, who lived in California, near San Francisco, returned to Britain only to find the very reasons for coming home had disappeared.

I was very close to my Nan, who was like a mother to me after my parents divorced when I was 16. I used to speak to her every day, even when I lived on the other side of the world. We had a lovely little routine. I would call her during our breakfast time and have a little chat.

Then she became ill with bowel cancer. I almost felt cut adrift because I was so far away. I couldn't even talk to her on the phone anymore. On top of this, my mother-in-law was very ill following a stroke. As a family we made the difficult decision to repatriate. We had a wonderful life in California, but family came first.

Less than five months after making that decision we were back in the UK. Unfortunately, a week before we returned, my Nan died. Two months later, my mother-in-law died.

It was heart breaking. The reason we had returned home was to spend time with them. I reconnected with friends locally and tried to get into a routine, but there has always been a longing to return to expat life. I wished we hadn't come back. After all, you can't control what's going to happen in the lives of others. To be honest we should have committed to expat life from the start. We should have sold our UK house and moved our home completely, otherwise there is always the feeling that expat life is temporary. It was exciting to come back, but the numbness soon set in. I'd lost close members of my family and in the process lost my home and lifestyle.

Meet Margaret

Margaret, an American who has lived in Oman and the UAE, was excited to be returning home. She missed her family and friends. She missed the familiarity of everything. And then she missed expat life.

I was so excited when my husband told me we were returning home. It had been really hard to leave my family when we first moved to Oman, and my friends thought I was mad to be moving to the Middle East at all.

I was looking forward to the freedom. I wanted to live in a house that I owned, not rented. I wanted a garden, where I could grow flowers, not just a giant sandpit. Most of all, I wanted to feel like I fitted in. I wasn't that I didn't enjoy my expat life. I loved it. It broadened my horizons and made me feel like an explorer. It was an opportunity to visit places I'd never heard of, let along dreamt about.

But life wasn't as I imagined it. Friends had moved on and I had to be really careful not to keep talking about my old life. It was something they couldn't relate to and it didn't really interest them. I get that. But when you're talking to friends you draw on your life experiences. Every sentence seemed to start "When I lived in…" before I trailed off, embarrassed that it would be judged as one-upmanship.

That's not to say I couldn't talk about it. I just decided that I wouldn't volunteer information. I figured that if people were interested they would ask.

I do love being home, but it took me longer than I anticipated to settle. While everything looked like I remembered, there were new stores or new technology that meant I just had to catch up a little. I was away for nine years. A lot happens.

They say the grass is always greener. Over time I forgot about the dust that I hated. I forgot about the red tape and the inability to get what I wanted from the grocery store. But I didn't forget the cocktail nights, or the beach, or the fun we had. I started to ache for my expat life.

I've made peace with all that now. It's not that I won't be able to travel again. I'm not shackled to the US. I can even live abroad again. Just not at the moment. It's great that I remember the good stuff. A good dose of reality means that I reassure myself that there will be pros and cons wherever I live. I need to stop chasing the pros. There isn't a place on the planet that doesn't have cons.

What other expats have to say

Jennifer, a Brit who has lived in the UAE and Oman
Leaving a country after a very long time can take a while to get used to. My mother went through a grieving process for a year when she left her [expat] home and friends behind after 17 years abroad.

Louise, a Brit who has lived in Spain, Australia, Malta and Dubai
I volunteer for an animal rescue group and it breaks my heart when we find animals dumped on the streets because their family has moved away and left them behind. Plan ahead, save up, take your whole family!

Alexandra, from Portugal, has lived in Brazil, Switzerland and Italy
We are now different from the ones that we left in our home town, so sometimes they call us "Swiss" because we are always on time for appointments! Or that we use our hands more when we speak, like Italians!

Patty, a Uruguayan who lives in the UK
People move on and learn to live without you. Some friendships remain but not all. Plus, a piece of your heart is left behind, which makes the repat process hard. You will never feel 100% at home again. Once a migrant…always a migrant.

Susan, an American living in the UK

It was difficult to find people who could understand our lives. [It's] Like trying to explain Narnia to people who just see a wardrobe.

Victoria, a Brit living in Singapore

We have been in Singapore for six years, and in the last 18 months many of our closest friends have moved away, to Italy, the UK and Dubai. This really shook our bedrock of support and is very unsettling. One begins to wonder if our time is up too. But this year, for Chinese New Year, we decided to make an impromptu trip to see our friends in Dubai and meet their new baby - their first.

We had a wonderful time as if no time or distance was between us. They have asked up to be godparents to their little girl. I am filled with pride, joy and gratitude for these friends and the opportunities expat life offers.

Allison, a Canadian who lived in Dubai

Repating was very difficult. I felt I had expanded my horizons when I was abroad and didn't fit in the mould I left. It was jarring to step back into the same, old conversations.

Where do you start?

- Find a support group. While your friends might not want to hear about your time abroad every time they see you, there are thousands of expats in the same situation. Facebook is a good place to start.

- Write a list of what you missed about your homeland and remind yourself of the advantages.

- Take the opportunity to see your homeland through the eyes of a tourist. Plan a holiday in your own country, or a staycation, that enables you to reconnect with your own culture.

Epilogue

I'm sitting in my study, finishing this book, or rather gazing through the window at the spring, which is just about to burst into flower. It's two and a half years since we came back from our last placement, but it already seems so long ago.

I have hundreds of happy memories filed away. I often flip through them in my mind. But every now and then I panic when I can't remember something. What was the road called where we went to that restaurant, the tapas one? I can't remember its name! How did I get the girls to school? Which way did I drive? What was the name of the neighbour I had coffee with a couple of times? I wonder what they are doing now.

At first, I thought I had early onset dementia. And then I realised, I have so many memories my brain can't cope. It's literally binned anything irrelevant. When I talk to other repats this seems to be a common experience. It makes us crave to go abroad again to check that things are as we remembered them.

That doesn't mean I'm not content. I've just learnt to understand that every experience has its merits. I no longer have to deal with the heat and humidity. But I've traded it for frost and shorter days in the winter. I can no longer wander the meandering paths of the botanical garden, with its exotic jungle plants. But that's been replaced by open countryside, green hills and blossom-lined roads. I no longer dress up to go to up-market hotels for cocktails. But I can walk to a country pub with a pretty garden and a decent roast dinner.

I've made a real effort to protect my memories as much as I can. The labours of late nights, putting photobooks together, are lined up neatly on the shelf. I may currently be living in my homeland, but I haven't retired from international exploration. There will be adventurous holidays in the future. When the children have finished their secondary education there may even be new homes in new countries. It's just exciting, and a relief, to know it's a possibility.

For now, I must remember to be content, appreciate the benefits of my current location, and gather family and friends around me. I hope you are happy in your home, wherever you are.

Appendix

Expat statistics

Data from 675 respondents was collected over a two-year period from 2016-2018.

Question 1
Where are you from?

Top 5 locations:
44%	UK
15%	USA
11%	Australia
2%	India
2%	Ireland

This does not directly correlate with the actual number of migrants from each country. It is only a cross section of that community - people who were willing to be part of the survey.

There will also be biases. As I am British, a large proportion of my contacts are British. Although I have linked to the wider expat community, and didn't socialise just with Brits, there will always be a bias based on the survey origin. There is also bias based on the places I've lived – UK, USA, UAE and Singapore.

To enable the survey to be as unbiased as possible, people were encouraged to share it with people they knew. It was posted on global social media boards and pushed through international organisations. The result is a response from 675 people from 56 countries.

Respondent's birthplace:

Zimbabwe Bahrain Chile Ecuador Taiwan Philippines Columbia Gaza Strip Portugal Germany Belgium Mexico Denmark Hong Kong New Zealand Slovenia United Kingdom United Arab Emirates Australia Brazil Egypt Spain Finland Malaysia Argentina Netherlands South Africa Czech Republic Ireland Kenya Poland Estonia Ukraine Lithuania Slovakia United States Switzerland Romania Jamaica Turkey Italy Canada Serbia Costa Rica Nigeria India Malta France Uruguay Venezuela Sweden Dominican Republic Hungary Oman Norway Cameroon Pakistan Tunisia Russia

Question 2
Where do you live now?

Top 5 locations:
26%   UK
20%   Singapore
15%   UAE
6%   USA
4%   Australia

Respondent's current home:

Oman, Sweden, Italy, Uruguay, Ireland, Mexico, Nigeria, Belgium, Hungary, Slovenia, Zimbabwe, Malaysia, Ecuador, Romania, Venezuela, Lithuania, France, Costa Rica, United Arab Emirates, Czech Republic, South Africa, Netherlands, New Zealand, Finland, Canada, Philippines, Gaza Strip, Hong Kong, Portugal, Brazil, Taiwan, Poland, Kenya, Egypt, United States, Serbia, Spain, United Kingdom, Turkey, Dominican Republic, Russia, Argentina, Switzerland, Australia, Bahrain, Tunisia, Jamaica, Cameroon, Singapore, Pakistan, Chile, Estonia, Columbia, India, Slovakia, Denmark, Germany, Ukraine, Norway, Malta

Question 3
How old are you?

The results showed that the largest age group was 40-44, although there was a good spread of ages.

4% of respondents were under 30 (young professionals or students); 93% fell into the family bracket (aged 30-60) and 4% were over 60 and of retiree age.

There could be a slight bias in the data based on how respondents received the survey. For example, a larger number of younger people will have picked the survey up from social media.

Question 4
Who did you live with as an expat?

Given the age of the average expat, it's not surprising that most people live abroad with children. 60% of respondents lived with children with 34% living with their partner and two children. A third lived just with a partner. This may indicate parents with children who have fled the nest, or gone to boarding school, as well as younger couples yet to have children and older couples who chose not to have children. Essentially, it shows that children play a huge role in the expat theatre, and therefore the debate about how this type of life influences them is a positive one to have. 42% of expats are without children.

Question 5
How old were your children when you moved abroad?

60%	pre-school aged children
26%	primary school aged children

6%   secondary school aged children
7%   adult children

Looking deeper at the influence of expat life on children it is interesting to see that most couples moved abroad with very young children. The survey has shown that most people move due to career opportunities (66% question 14), which seems to come towards the middle of the career cycle. This also coincides with the time life partners have children.

The likelihood of moving abroad tails off the older respondents get, potentially influenced by education options. Parents with older children will be older themselves, and so further along in their career, i.e. people are less likely to move abroad the older they are, or less likely to disrupt their children's secondary education.

Question 6
How many years have you lived aboard?

People seem to get the expat bug. Of course, there are plenty of stories of people desperate to return home. However, the statistics suggest the average (mode) length of stay abroad is five to 10 years (29%). Only 4% of expats returned home after a year.

Question 7
How many countries have you lived in?

The survey indicates that most expats don't move to one place – around 80% of expats have lived in two or more countries. Opportunities to move appear to be greater once you become an expat, particular in countries with labour or skills shortages. One expat surveyed has lived in ten countries.

Only 19% have only lived in one country; 30% have lived in two; 26% have lived in three; 11% have lived in four; 13% have lived in more than five countries.

Question 8
Where have you lived?

Qatar, Spain, Kenya, Norway, Zambia, Canada, Germany, Morocco, Malta, Serbia, Hungary, Zimbabwe, Bahrain, Slovenia, Chile, Kuwait, Pakistan, Austria, Brunei, Cameroon, Netherlands, Ethiopia, Romania, Taiwan, Brazil, Sri Lanka, Costa Rica, Lithuania, Japan, Italy, Luxembourg, Argentina, Ecuador, Gaza Strip, United Arab Emirates, Dominican Republic, France, Indonesia, Czech Republic, United Kingdom, Poland, India, Cambodia, Saudi Arabia, United States, Nigeria, Belgium, Hong Kong, Philippines, New Zealand, Jamaica, Russia, Ukraine, Ireland, South Africa, Singapore, Switzerland, Cyprus, Malaysia, Portugal, Australia, Denmark, Venezuela, Slovakia, Uganda, Columbia, Estonia, Tunisia, Thailand, Uruguay, Sweden, Finland, Mexico, Egypt, Vietnam, China, Turkey, Oman

Question 9
Did you move with your job or are you the "trailing spouse"?

Most people who answered the survey moved abroad with their partner's job (54%). 25% moved with their own job. The *other* category includes people who moved with their parents, those who moved to one country with their partner's job and moved again with their job, or vice versa, and those who moved without a job for a lifestyle change or to look for work.

Question 10
What sector do you/ does your partner work in?

If most people move abroad due to work opportunities (66% question 14) it's interesting to note the types of careers that promote global mobilisation. The three biggest single sectors represented were financial services (15%), oil and gas (11%) and professional services (8%). Aviation, manufacturing, education, construction and hospitality feature highly.

Question 11
Did you have to learn a new language?

English is a language spoken all over the world. With this in mind, there will be a bias in the results as this is an English language survey, and so respondents will already speak English. If they can make themselves understood in English, there is less pressure to learn a new language. Just under 70% of respondents replied that they did not have to learn a new language.

It is interesting to note the languages that were learnt.

Spanish Mandarin Dutch Portuguese Serbian Japanese Cantonese Italian Russian Turkish Thai Swedish Greek German French Bahasa English Hindi Arabic

Question 12
How long did it take you to feel settled?

It appears to take most people between six and 12 months to feel settled (31%); 19% took between three and six months; For 23% the process took more than a year. Some people (6%) never feel settled. This can contribute to expats returning home early, or unhappiness if they stay.

Question 13
What do you miss most about home?

How quickly someone settles is as much about what they have left behind, as it is about getting to grips with their new surroundings. Missing family and friends were the top reasons respondents cited for missing home (62% combined). 47% missed family, 15% cited friends, 10% stated countryside, 3% said weather. A further 2% missed their working life.

Question 14
Why did you move?

Unsurprisingly, the main reason people move to a new country is for work opportunities (66%), either with their job or their partner's - 43% moved due their partners' job prospects and 23% moved due to their own job prospects. Just over 13% moved for a cultural experience and 6% moved for financial reasons.

Push factors included escaping politics or earthquakes. Pull factors included searching for a better quality of life and moving to be with a partner of a different nationality.

Question 15
Do you think that children benefit from expat life?

Overwhelmingly, most people (97%) felt children did benefit from a life abroad. Reasons given included learning new languages, broadening views, developing flexibility, understanding diversity, and growing up with an accepting multi-cultural view of the world.

Question 16
Do you think that children are disadvantaged by expat life?

Although most respondents (97%) felt children benefitted from expat life, a number of disadvantages were noted too by 49% of respondents.

Reasons included lack of stability leading to an inability to settle, distant relationships with family in country of origin, cultural difficulties i.e. not being able to identify with their country of origin, and in some cases living a spoilt or sheltered lifestyle.

Question 17
Does expat life make you financially better off?

Most people (63%) felt their financial position had improved due to expat life. Near 14% said there weren't financially better off and 24% weren't sure.

Question 18
Have you found it easy to make friends?

More than three quarters (76%) of respondents found it easy to make friends because they found expat communities to be open and friendly with others in the same situation. Having children was also noted as a way to make friends through schools and activity groups.

However, a distinction was made between countries that have large expat communities (e.g. Dubai, Singapore) compared to communities where expats are more integrated (e.g. USA, UK). It is easier to make friends with other expats, and harder to make friends when you're seen as transient.

It was also highlighted that you make deeper friendships more quickly with other expats, due to the transient nature of expat life, not knowing when you'll be moving to a new country again.

Question 19
Please rank the advantages of being an expat

The top three reasons were cultural experience (32%), being financially better off (26%) and travel (16%).

Question 20
Please rank the disadvantages of being an expat

The three top disadvantages were being away from friends and family (57%), the physical distance from home (21%) and legal restrictions (10%).

Question 21
If you could have your experience again what would you do differently?

These answers were very personal with a massive range of subjects. Themes that reoccurred, however, include travel more; save more;

learn the language; do more research into the destination; negotiate a better package with employer.

Probably the best testament to expat life is the repeated comment that the respondent would have done it earlier.

Question 22
What words of advice do you have for new expats about moving, making friends, settling children, staying sane…?

The advice and information from this section of the survey has been quoted throughout the book.

The reoccurring themes included keeping an open mind; saying yes to every positive opportunity; having patience and giving yourself time; making friends; joining clubs; and absorbing the local culture.

Question 23
Did you find it difficult to repat (move back home)?

Nearly half of all expats (48%) find it difficult to return home. There are many reasons for this, but one issue is that the image expats have of home may be different from reality – you can't just slot back in.

Respondents found it hard to connect with people who didn't have the same experiences or broaden world view. They found that friendships had changed and moved on, even if they'd made the effort to stay in contact while apart. This was either because friends had moved on, or the respondent themselves had changed.

Question 24
What words of advice do you have for expats moving back home?

Again, the responses to this question have been quoted throughout the book. General themes include trying not to compare things; understand that you might have changed while others haven't; prepare as if it's another posting; don't expect things to be the same.

Expat extra

While I've weaved insights from expats throughout this book, here are a couple of extra gems.

The good

- *I worked on my husband for almost a decade to move overseas. Then Trump got elected and he was all on board. Now he really likes it here, can step back and see the US with distance. He isn't sure he ever wants to move back. We miss our families, but it's been incredible for our immediate family.*

- *A group of friends from the UK gave me a "bag of thoughts" and messages to take aboard. The idea was that whenever I felt homesick I could open a message, or play a CD etc. I found that just thinking of this bag of treasures was enough to cheer me and I ended up keeping them until the great sadness of leaving to come home.*

- *People who are virtual strangers will go the extra mile for you, as everyone appreciates you are away from your family.*

- *Be careful: your expat children are likely to end up expats themselves. I did, and so did many of my friends. It's contagious! People tend to say expat life is not "normal" and that we live in a bubble. For me, this is normal, and I know no other life and love it.*

The bad

- My container, with the contents of my entire home, disappeared overboard. It was an insurance nightmare as it was a shared container, and I was told my name wasn't listed. My advice is use your own insurance not your shipper's unless they are a reputable company.

- I ran a boutique hotel in Hong Kong that had one toaster that always popped up too soon, the bread barely warm. We took it apart to fix it and out strolls a rather fat gecko, who had obviously crawled in when he was very tiny.

- When you are the expat wife, you've left everything. Sometimes you feel that you should be baking cookies or cleaning all the time. You have to fight to remember who you really are; [you're] not only "the backpack".

- I was a passenger in a friend's car. The driver had arrived in Singapore two years before. She didn't know the directions, missed the turn and then proceeded down the wrong side of the street.

- It's difficult watching your youngest struggling to answer the apparently simple question: "Where do you come from?"

The bizarre

- After six months in Paris, I asked a waiter in French for water. His face dropped as what I'd actually said was "I would like you".

- I ran over the foot of the ruler of Dubai with a shopping trolley from Carrefour.

- I remember sitting down and eating with locals. All the parts of *the sheep were there – eye ball, other balls, brain. I was too polite to refuse.*

- *For the first few months of being in Italy I told everyone "I only speak to little Italian" rather than only speaking a little Italian – fairly amusing considering I'm over six feet tall.*

- *I lived in Kuwait until I was six and used to visit my grandparents in England. I used to think all the young people and children lived in Kuwait and only old wrinkly people lived in England!*

- *In Fiji, my children used to take their shoes off when they got to school. When we moved to Singapore my youngest questioned the principal in the new school. He said: "Shoes and socks all day?! Why is this?" The principal could give her no answer.*

- *I have lots of fond memories of my time in China, although it was a little strange when Chinese women tried to "help" me when breastfeeding in public!*

Interview with my children

When my children were seven and five, I interviewed them to see if their expat experience had changed the way they saw the world.

Madeleine was three when we first moved abroad to Chicago, and Tilda was six-months-old.

They were five and two when we moved to Dubai, and seven and four when we moved to Singapore.

Madeleine (age seven):

Diaper or nappy?
Diaper

Courgette or zucchini?
Courgette

Eggplant or aubergine?
Aubergine

What do you want to be when you grow up?
Fashion designer

If religion is about praying to a god, how do you pray?
You relax your head on a pillow and reach up and turn your hands over and go up and down.

Where do you pray?

Some people do it in mosques, some people do it in churches and some people do it in temples. It's because they have different religions. People live in different places with different traditions.

What is a country?
It's a part of the world. It has a flag. They are all different shapes and sizes. They have different religions. They have different things inside the country. Egypt has pyramids and France doesn't. England has Big Ben and Germany doesn't.

What else is different?
There are different languages. We look different. We do different jobs. Each country has different money too.

You were born in the UK. What do you like about the UK?
I like Big Ben and I like going to see my relatives and friends.

What do you like about living abroad?
I like exploring different countries. I like learning new things and exploring buildings especially tall ones. My favourite building is the Burj Khalifa (Dubai) and my second favourite is the Hancock Tower (Chicago).

Where would you like to live next and why?
France because I want to see the Eiffel Tower. I went there when I was a baby, but I was too small to remember it.

Tilda (age five):

Diaper or nappy?
Nappy

Courgette or zucchini?
Courgette

Eggplant or aubergine?
Eggplant

What do you want to be when you grow up?
Ballerina

If religion is about praying to god, how do you pray?
It's like having a rest (to demonstrate she bows down on the floor).

Where do you pray?
Where you see statues.

What is a country?
It has a flag.

What else is different?
Dubai was very hot. And some countries are not.

You were born in the UK. What do you like about the UK?
My family.

Where would you like to live next and why?
Australia because it's my favourite country because I used to have a friend from Australia, and I want to see him. But I don't know what his name is now.

www.expatexplorers.org
www.facebook.com/expatexplorers
www.pinterest.com/expatexplorers
www.twitter.com/expatexplorers

Helen McClure
helen@expatexplorers.org

Amanda, an American living in the UK:
This is a thought-provoking, real-world guide to expat life: the adventure, challenges, exhilaration, and hiccups of it all. It's a relatable, funny and thoughtful account of the realities of life abroad, full of great advice for newbies and vets alike!

Claire, a Brit who lived in Singapore:
This book is great for anyone who feels alone on their expat journey. It's reassuring and really gives you a boost to help you realise you're not the only one.

Printed in Poland
by Amazon Fulfillment
Poland Sp. z o.o., Wrocław